Forged in *Armor,*

Freed by *Love*

FORGED IN ARMOR, FREED BY LOVE

A Raw Journey Through Trauma, Truth, Awakening, and the Return to Wholeness

Geoffrey Costa

Published by Game Changer Publishing

Paperback ISBN: 978-1-968250-11-9

Hardcover ISBN: 978-1-968250-12-6

Digital ISBN: 978-1-968250-13-3

GC GAME CHANGER
PUBLISHING
www.GameChangerPublishing.com

For my children—who consistently gave me the reason to rise again.

And for my wife, Kathryn—my sacred partner in purpose,
and my divine reminder that every step inward leads
to the greatest gifts waiting to be received.

READ THIS FIRST

Just to say thanks for buying and reading my book,
I would like to connect with you!
Scan the QR Code Here:

Forged in *Armor,* Freed by *Love*

A Raw Journey Through Trauma, Truth, Awakening, and the Return to Wholeness

Geoffrey Costa

.

FOREWORD

The release of this book could not come at a better time in the world. Right now, as a species, we are collectively undergoing a metamorphosis. We are being asked to shed the old to make way for the new. To leave behind the old stories, patterns, and behaviors that are weighing us down, to uncover our gold. The process is not easy. It is rocky, full of potholes along the way, and does not come with a roadmap to the destination. Sure, it's a challenging geography to navigate, but can you think of any other adventure better suited for the evolution of the human soul?

It's fascinating. When we look at nature, our greatest teacher, she points us toward a great truth. Decay is required for the growth of new life. Like magic, decomposing plant material transforms into the essential nutrients needed for new life. In this way, death becomes a holy intervention. If nature could speak, or perhaps if we could better listen, I think she might remind us that we are one and the same. That her cycles hold up a mirror to our own. And that living in accordance with nature's laws, rather than resisting them, is the key to our growth. Rather than anxiously holding onto our rotting leaves at the end of a season, we would graciously drop them, allowing the death of the old to make way for the new.

Close your eyes. Just for a moment, listen. What parts of you are exhausted from the constant gripping to an identity that is no longer YOU? Are they aching to be laid to rest? Sure, it's painful to sit with the implications of what it might mean to say goodbye while embarking on a pathless path. But it's worth it—I promise. Our growth requires sacrifice. It is a willingness to fall apart into decay, watching what is no longer true crumble before our eyes, all while continuing to show up, no matter how long the transformation takes. We must be willing to fill our hearts with as much courage as we can muster and look the devil right in the eye, in the fiercest staring contest anyone has ever seen. Then and only then can we dissolve the barriers keeping us in rot.

In this book, Geoffrey takes us through a powerful first-hand account of his own personal hero's journey. From the grips of depression, PTSD, and sexual abuse, Geoffrey shares a very real and intimate inside look at his own personal road to healing. His message is loud and clear and will leave an impact that not only changes the way you look at your own life processes, but the way you choose to engage with them. Geoffrey's roadmap—essential tools for self-inquiry and a heartfelt perspective —offers readers something invaluable: a perspective shift and opportunity toward a new chance at life.

– *Victoria Wueschner*
Co-Founder & Educator at F.I.V.E.
(5-MeO-DMT Information & Vital Education)
Facilitator & Director of Education at Tandava Retreats

CONTENTS

ACKNOWLEDGMENTS   1

INTRODUCTION   3

1. THE FAÇADE OF A PERFECT LIFE   5

2. FINDING A NEW FAMILY: THE MILITARY   15

3. FROM BATTLEFIELD TO HOME FRONT: THE DUAL STRUGGLE   27

4. THE BREAKING POINT   43

5. CHOOSING TO FIGHT FOR MY LIFE   51

6. REBUILDING THROUGH CONNECTION, SPORTS, SERVICE, AND SHOWING UP   61

7. THE LESSONS OF THE HORSE: HEALING THROUGH EQUINE THERAPY   71

8. BREAKING THE EGO: A SPIRITUAL AWAKENING   81

9. LOVE, EXPANSION, AND THE NEXT CHAPTER   95

10. THE BUSINESS JOURNEY BEGINS   109

11. GOLD NUGGETS OF WISDOM: CHOOSING PEACE, PURPOSE, AND TRUE FULFILLMENT   119

CONCLUSION   129

THANK YOU FOR READING MY BOOK!   133

ACKNOWLEDGMENTS

This book is a product of pain, growth, surrender, and love, but it was never a journey I took alone.

To my children, you are the light that brought me out of the darkness. Your love, presence, and laughter gave me reasons to keep fighting, even on the days I didn't feel worthy of breath. Everything I've done, everything I've rebuilt, is for you. I pray that you walk through life unburdened by the weight of my past and are, instead, lifted by the wings of my healing.

To my wife, thank you for seeing me, not the masks, not the medals, but *me.* Your love came at a time when I had finally begun to love myself. You didn't complete me—you met me in my wholeness, and together, we rise. Together, we conquer all. The present and the future are ours. I love you endlessly.

To my ex-wife, thank you. Thank you for your presence throughout so many chapters of my life. Thank you for being the one to plant the seed that led me to Tandava Retreats and helped change the trajectory of my healing. Our children and our growth will always be sacred.

To my family, for all that was and all that wasn't, thank you. You were human, and so was I. The journey to understanding and reflection has shown me that we all carry pain, but we all also carry the capacity to grow. I carry forward the love, the lessons, and the chance to break the cycle.

To Joël and Victoria, and also to Luis and Otto of Tandava Retreats, thank you for creating a container that allowed my soul to breathe for the first time. You offered me space, safety, and the invitation to remember who I truly am. No words can ever describe my gratitude and love for you.

To the Warrior Ranch family, Eileen Shanahan and Juliette, and every volunteer and veteran I've shared the pen with, thank you for reminding me that healing can happen in stillness, through presence, and in the sacred silence between a human and a horse.

To Fiona, you were the first glimpse, the calm in the chaos. I didn't understand it then, but I do now.

To the West Point Lacrosse Brotherhood and my fellow veterans, thank you for giving me a space to belong again, for reminding me that I am not alone in the fight, and for proving that brotherhood and sister-hood don't end when the uniform comes off.

To the reader, thank you. You gave me your time, your trust, and your heart. I hope this story is more than just words—I hope it is a mirror, a breath, and a call to come home to yourself.

And finally, to the divine intelligence that guides all things, thank you for never leaving me, even when I left myself.

There are no ordinary moments.

INTRODUCTION

*I wrote this book for the person
who feels like they've tried everything...
and still feels lost.*

I am a combat veteran, corporate leader, father, business owner, and a survivor of my own worst battles. I have faced war, trauma, loss, depression, and the slow unraveling of identity when life no longer makes sense. This book is the story of how I fought my way back—not by chasing success, but by learning how to come home to myself.

I wrote this book to share the lessons I've learned so that others can find their path to healing and purpose. I want to help those struggling with identity, purpose, and self-worth know that they are not alone.

It's for anyone who's ever asked, *"Is this all there is?"*

It's for the athlete chasing performance, the veteran searching for peace, the professional wearing the mask of success while quietly unraveling inside. It's for anyone who feels disconnected from who they really are.

Why should you listen to me? The short answer is that I lived it. I survived the darkest moments and rebuilt my life. I understand what it means to feel lost, but I also know how to find the way back.

This isn't a book of theories or clichés. It's a raw, unfiltered story of falling apart—and the path I took to rise again with clarity, peace, and purpose. It's part memoir, part mirror, part roadmap for anyone who's ready to stop surviving and start truly living.

My hope is that these words remind you of what's already alive inside you: the power to choose again, to rise again, to begin again.

And so, my story begins—not at the peak, but at rock bottom.

Long before I ever understood what survival truly meant.

CHAPTER 1
THE FAÇADE OF A PERFECT LIFE

THE LOSS OF MY FATHER

was just three years old when my father took his own life.

At that age, you don't understand what death means, let alone suicide. However, without even understanding it, the absence becomes a presence, a silence that you feel through every milestone, every father-son moment that never happened. For years, I believed my father had died from a brain aneurysm.

That's what my mom told me. It wasn't until my 13th birthday that she sat my older brother and me down and revealed to us the truth: that our father had died by suicide. That moment was very dramatic, and she chose my 13th birthday because, as she declared, I was now "old enough to know the truth."

It was jarring, an ambush disguised as her giving us truth or a revelation. I remember sitting in her bedroom in shock, not just from this truth that she had just shared, but from the weight of having lived in her lie for a decade.

As a child, I had internalized her version of the story so deeply that every time I had a headache, I feared I might be dying of a brain aneurysm. So, her lie hadn't protected me; it had haunted me. When the truth came out, it felt like the already unstable foundation that I had been standing on had cracked beneath me.

My mom said that she had been trying to shield us from that hurtful reality, but it felt much more like another layer of betrayal. You see, as I will share more about later, I was already a child tormented by sexual and physical abuse, and now I had to deal with this. This moment reshaped my relationship with my mom. It reshaped how I trusted her, and it reshaped how I saw the truth.

My mom remarried not long after my father's death. From the outside, it looked like we were a normal family again, but on the inside, the story was much more complex. Overall, my stepfather was a good man. He stepped into a challenging situation, marrying a woman with two young boys after never having had children of his own. He was also carrying his own childhood trauma. He had no real parental role model to draw from, and he was navigating a role he hadn't fully asked for or been prepared to take on.

My stepfather led with tough love. "Don't tell me you love me—show me you love me by taking out the garbage," he would say. His version of discipline often came through the snap of a belt, passed down from a generation that believed that fear built character. At dinner, he'd lecture us about how his father used to strike him for something as small as the sound of a fork tapping against his teeth. And yet, he never missed a single one of my games, and he was always behind the camera, recording every moment for me. He was a living paradox: a man trying to be better than his father but still lost in the shadow of what manhood was supposed to look like. Misguided but not malicious. Flawed but not absent.

Before he and my mom had their own child—my younger brother, born eight years after me—my stepfather often used our alone time, especially during car rides, to vent his frustrations. It was as if I were his thera-

FORGED IN ARMOR, FREED BY LOVE

pist. He would tell me why he didn't feel capable of being a better dad or making firmer decisions amidst the chaos. He'd say things like, "You have to understand, I am not your actual father. I feel like the rest of the family is overly involved, so I step back. If I had my own child, I would do things differently."

Eventually, he did. When my younger brother was born, I saw a shift in how my stepfather showed up as a parent. And with that shift came an even heavier pressure for me to keep the peace, avoid mistakes, and not add to the dysfunction that already lived in our home.

My older brother's presence in the home added yet another layer of tension. His relationship with our mom was deeply strained and often volatile. He carried a lot of anger, while my mom bore the weight of unresolved grief and wounds of her own. Their constant conflicts would often escalate to the point of explosion, leaving me to step in as an emotional shield. I became the buffer, absorbing the blows, both emotional and physical, in a desperate attempt to protect her from the storm. At just 14, I was thrust into a role no child should have to bear, trying to mend a broken family dynamic.

When my brother was removed from the house and placed into a church setting, there was a collective sigh of relief, a belief that this was the answer, the solution to our troubles. It was assumed that removing him would mend the fractures, that getting him help would bring peace.

However, the silence left behind, while a relief, was also a stark reminder of the unresolved pain that lingered. My mom's grief, my step-dad's unhealed traumas, and the heavy responsibility I carried did not dissipate with his absence. It became evident that the removal was merely a band-aid on a deeper wound, one that no quick fix could heal.

LIVING IN A HOUSE THAT WASN'T A HOME

I was sexually and physically abused by a family member—an act that shattered any sense of safety I had as a child. The betrayal wasn't just physical; it broke something deep inside me. It was as if my body no longer belonged to me.

In that confusion, silence became my survival strategy. I didn't have the words. I didn't have the safety to speak them. That silence marked the beginning of my first mask, one I would wear for decades. It would layer itself beneath a growing storm of questions, insecurities, and instability, all compounded by the suicide of my father.

On the outside, we looked like the perfect suburban family. My mom was the "cool" mom—friendly, charismatic, and loved by my friends. My female friends would call the house just to talk to her. She hosted pasta dinners for my football team, summer pool parties, and New Year's Eve gatherings. Extended family members and neighbors saw warmth, laughter, and hospitality, but behind the curated smiles and holiday cheer, our house held secrets.

Our home was more a place of performance than one of peace. It was a stage, not a sanctuary. Appearances mattered more than authenticity. Everything needed to look normal, even when nothing felt normal. Inside that spotless home, silence screamed. Guests would compliment the decor and sip wine while I stood quietly in the corner, numb to their smiles. The laughter from the dinner table didn't reach the hallway, where I cried alone.

On the outside, we were the perfect family. On the inside, we were a war zone dressed in pressed khakis and Sunday shoes. I became an expert at pretending, at smiling on cue, at making straight A's while carrying invisible wounds. The fear didn't scream; it whispered. It showed up in the sound of footsteps, in praying that a day would pass without an altercation with my mom and brother, in the pause before dinner, in hoping my fork wouldn't clink too loudly against my teeth, in the invisible pressure to be perfect, obedient, emotionless.

Generational trauma ran deep in my family. The pain wasn't new—it was inherited, passed down through discipline, denial, and emotional distance through disconnection disguised as discipline. Pain didn't start with us, but it lived with us. As a young boy, I made a promise that I wouldn't fully understand for years:

The cycle ends with me.

I will see my children.

I will hear my children.

I will protect them.

I will choose connection over control.

I will build a home, not a stage.

SURVIVAL MODE: THE MASK I WORE

In the middle of all the chaos, I found a strategy: be perfect. I became the ideal son, the reliable student, the committed athlete. I wore those roles like armor. They kept me invisible to the dysfunction around me and gave me a sense of worth when everything else felt unstable. I also wanted to be the answer for my family to be happy. I wanted to make life as easy as possible for them.

Overachievement became my camouflage. If I could just do everything right—get straight A's, win games, follow rules—maybe no one would notice the pain I carried. Maybe I wouldn't notice it, either.

I was a three-sport athlete—football, wrestling, and lacrosse. I poured myself into every season, chasing individual accolades and team success. I was named all-county, served as team captain, broke high school records, and was eventually inducted into my high school's sports hall of fame. But my performance didn't stop on the field. I sang in NYSSMA choir competitions, starred as the lead in school plays, and made sure I was seen as the one who had it all together.

This drive for perfection trickled into life outside of school, too. I would take my neighbors' trash cans to the curb and bring them back to their garage. I'd mow their lawns—without being asked. It wasn't just about being helpful; doing these things gave me one more reason to stay away from my house. The physical activity gave me a sense of control, of usefulness, and it fed the already abundant external validation I constantly sought in everything I did.

Sports became my escape. On the field, I could breathe. I'd stay long after practice ended, running drills alone in the fading light, pushing myself past exhaustion. There was a strange comfort in that physical pain —it was mine. It didn't come from someone else's hands. It gave me control. It gave me peace. That ache in my muscles was a reminder that I could still feel something on my own terms. The burn in my lungs, the sting of sweat in my eyes—those sensations grounded me. They were a language my body spoke when the rest of my world felt silent or chaotic.

At a very young age, I knew things weren't right, but I didn't know how to fix them. I tried to the best of my ability to *make* things right through my strategy of being perfect, of being the opposite of what everybody else was around me.

I carried my pain in silence, unsure about where to put it, who would listen, and who would believe me if I spoke. When I tried to approach my mom about certain things, she always said the same thing to me: "I lost my husband, the love of my life. I lost my sister. I am not going to lose your brother or anyone else." However, through my mom's inability to heal herself and deal with her own grief, she did lose someone. She lost me.

Maybe you are the kind of person who always has it together, the person people look up to, the strong one, but what happens when the strong one is struggling? I spent years burying my pain, thinking that if I just worked harder, pushed myself further, I could outrun it. But pain does not disappear. It waits.

If you're carrying something heavy, I want you to know this: you don't have to pretend to be okay. The real strength isn't in hiding. It's in healing.

So, I challenge you: what masks are you wearing today? Do you cope with pain by hiding, performing, or pushing yourself to the edge? What might healing look like if you finally took the mask off?

*Even in chaos, a door appeared, one that led far from
the house I grew up in and into a world built on discipline,
structure, and honor. That door was West Point—
and I believed it was my ticket out.*

KEY TAKEAWAYS FROM CHAPTER 1

- **Pain has a ripple effect** – Generational trauma isn't born with us, but it lives through us until someone chooses to stop the cycle.
- **Perfection is not protection** – Performing for approval or hiding behind success doesn't heal our wounds; it only buries them deeper.
- **Home isn't a place, it's a feeling** – True safety isn't built by appearances; it's built by connection, presence, and emotional safety.
- **Silence isn't strength** – True courage comes when we face the pain we've spent a lifetime trying to outrun.
- **You are not what happened to you** – You are who you *choose* to become on the other side of your story.

YOUR REFLECTION CHALLENGE

Sit with these questions—not to fix them all at once, but to open a doorway of awareness and truth:

1. What "masks" are you currently wearing to hide your pain or appear "put together"?

   _____

   _____

   _____

2. Where in your life are you performing for approval instead of standing in your Truth?

   _____

   _____

   _____

3. What unspoken stories from your past are you still carrying that deserve to be named and faced?

   _____

   _____

   _____

4. What cycle are you being invited to break—for yourself and for those who come after you?

_____

_____

_____

5. What does "home" actually mean to you? What would it feel like to live in a home—not a stage?

_____

_____

_____

You don't have to have all the answers today.
You just have to start by telling yourself the truth.

CHAPTER 2
FINDING A NEW FAMILY: THE MILITARY

THE TICKET OUT OF A BROKEN HOME

T o the world, The United States Military Academy at West Point is a crucible of leadership and discipline. To me, it was the first place that promised structure when all I had known was chaos. It's a place that has produced some of America's most distinguished military leaders and U.S. presidents. Its reputation is built on rigorous academics, intense physical training, and uncompromising ethical standards.

Acceptance into West Point is no small feat. The selection process is highly competitive, requiring not only academic excellence but also physical prowess, leadership potential, and a deep commitment to service. For me, it represented a new beginning—a chance to find a new family and purpose far from the turmoil of my home life. It wasn't just a prestigious opportunity; it was an escape. An escape from a broken home, from silence, from secrets. West Point represented everything my life hadn't been: stability, respect, structure. It wasn't just a dream come true. It was survival in a new form.

The moment I received my acceptance letter, it felt like my ticket out, a bridge to a life of structure and opportunity. Being accepted as an Army lacrosse player added another layer of pride and commitment, a sense of belonging and identity that I had been yearning for.

West Point provided me with a chance to redefine my future and escape the shadows of my past. I wasn't just joining the military. I was running toward something I had longed for my whole life up until this point: order, regiment, brotherhood, a place to belong.

Growing up in a home where safety didn't exist and love was conditional, I had already taught myself discipline. I had self-imposed routines to survive. I clung to structure like a life raft. West Point didn't scare me. It sharpened me. It refined all the tools that I already had, what I had already built. All the things that I used to bury and hide my pain, it refined for me.

Part of what opened the door to West Point was lacrosse. I was a recruited athlete, earning a spot on a Division I team. That gave me a new identity, not just as a cadet at West Point but now as a Division I athlete.

I got to be a warrior on the field. Many students at the academy were just adjusting to the academic lifestyle and military rigor, but I was also pushing myself to perform athletically at the highest level.

This also came with a great deal of stress. It was like the perfect trifecta of pressure: academic, military, and athletic performance. It also meant that I had no time for stillness.

It left no space to reflect. It left no quiet time. Every hour of the day was scheduled, and that was perfect for me.

STRUCTURE, DISCIPLINE, IDENTITY

West Point gave me what my childhood never could: clear expectations.

It gave me a daily structure. It gave me validation that came from excellence. My worth wasn't a question anymore.

It was measurable. My identity became performance-based, and I thrived on that. I became exactly who they wanted me to be.

From the outside, the rigid schedules and unbreakable rules looked like discipline. To me, they felt like safety. The physical demands, the constant pressure, the uniformity—all of it drowned out the inner noise I still didn't know how to face.

No one asked about my past. No one saw the wounds beneath the crisp uniform. I was thriving by every visible standard—but I was still hiding. Now, though, I was doing it with rank and salutes. I already knew how to shapeshift, so this was perfect for me. But behind every salute and every achievement, there was still the boy who hadn't healed. I just thought that if I could excel enough, if I could outrun the past, maybe I wouldn't have to feel what still lived inside me.

Being a cadet at West Point while also being a D1 athlete on the lacrosse team meant something deeper. It meant belonging to a team that represented more than just a sport. We represented resilience. We represented the warrior ethos. We represented grit. We represented tradition. We represented legacy. The Army lacrosse motto is family, toughness, tradition.

We didn't just play for wins. We played for a purpose, and that meant everything to us. That team kept me grounded during some of the most mentally and physically exhausting years of my life.

It was also a place that held its own pain, exemplified by a pivotal moment in my "Firstie" (senior) year. I was elected team captain of the Army lacrosse team—an honor akin to being a "captain of captains." However, this recognition was swiftly overshadowed. My head coach, citing my academic struggles, overrode the team's vote and opted for another player. That moment lingered, casting a shadow over my senior year and relegating me from team captain to backup player.

Another challenging memory from my time at West Point was my graduation. The prestigious moment that every cadet dreams of— throwing our dress uniform hats into the air as we hear "class dismissed" —was something I looked forward to. However, due to my academic struggles, my course load was shifted to summer school, and I missed that iconic moment. Instead of standing with my classmates and lacrosse brothers, celebrating the culmination of years of hard work, I had to wait for a separate ceremony. This left a lingering feeling of unfulfillment.

EMBRACING THE SUCK & THE LOSS OF MY SPIRITUALITY

While the Army built my body and hardened my will, it slowly chipped away at my spirit. For a lot of people, entering the military is a shock, but for me, it was very familiar.

Shouting and the need to perform were oddly comforting. There was no time to think, no time to reflect, no time to feel anything, and I loved that. The absence of stillness meant I never had to sit with my thoughts.

"Embracing the suck" is a term frequently used in the Army, and it didn't just stop at boot camp. My entire eleven-year journey through West Point and in the Army became an extended exercise of that endurance. The physical demands, the mental fortitude, and the emotional suppression all became just a part of that uniform that I wore, the armor that I was continuing to build around me as a person.

I hid behind the uniform, standing tall in my role, masking my own anticipation beneath rigid professionalism. I rose quickly in rank. I made the All-Army Fight Team. I was a two-time combatives champion. I volunteered for missions in Iraq I didn't have to be on and was praised for my courage. The Army rewarded performance, and I knew how to perform.

I will always remember rising at 4:30 a.m. in freezing temperatures for physical training, lacing up my boots in silence, steeling myself for another day of expectations, and I dared not ever fail. I would walk across the quad with my head held high and chest out, perfect posture, but with my heart locked away.

I was born and raised Catholic, but my faith became hard to hold on to as a soldier and even more so in combat. When you're constantly preparing for death, yours or someone else's, you learn to compartmentalize. God became an afterthought, and the goal became survival, but it wasn't just combat that created a spiritual erosion.

I was a freshman at West Point, which they call your plebe year, on September 11, 2001. The day our world changed forever. I was sitting in class when we got the word that the planes had hit the towers.

At that moment, everything shifted. We knew our purpose at West Point had changed. We weren't just cadets anymore. We were future warriors. We were going to war. Our class became known as the class of 9/11.

We were the first class to enter West Point in a time of peace and graduate in a time of war. By our senior year, 2005, we were actually on the cover of *Time* magazine as the class of 9/11, a symbol of the next generation of officers stepping into an uncertain, violent world.

No matter how much West Point trained us, and it trained us well, there was no manual, no course, no professor, and no officer who could have fully prepared us to graduate from college and then immediately be tasked with leading soldiers into war. The emotional and spiritual toll is something no one talks about until it's far too late.

War demanded that I shut off parts of my humanity, parts of my soul, to function as a leader. It hardened me in ways I wouldn't understand until much later. I learned to lead with courage and command but never with vulnerability. Emotions had no place on the battlefield. I disconnected from my soul because it was the only way to survive. The things I had to do in Iraq, the things that I witnessed, were things that I was not ready to face, especially in terms of spirituality.

I remember deployments to Iraq where I couldn't afford to flinch, as lives were on the line. I remember aches in my chest when I would receive letters from home that I had no idea how to respond to. That sucked, but embracing the suck became my normal.

I didn't just survive it; I made it my identity. I prided myself on how much I could endure, and the more I endured, the more praise I received.

But no one praised the silent suffering underneath.

CARRYING THE WEIGHT OF COMMAND & EMOTIONAL DISCONNECTION AT HOME

When I deployed to Iraq as the commanding officer, I carried not only the weight of leading soldiers into combat, but also the quiet ache of what I had left behind. Traditionally, the spouse of a commander steps up to lead the Family Readiness Group, or FRG, back home, supporting the families of those deployed. But my ex-wife didn't want that responsibility. She didn't want to be the one holding it all together for anyone else when she felt like she was barely holding it together herself. And I couldn't blame her. We were young, scared, and facing another chapter of separation. She was pregnant, alone, and overwhelmed. So, she made the decision to move back to New York to be near family, leaving our house at Fort Sill, OK dark, silent, and empty.

It felt like two deployments at once—one overseas, leading soldiers into the unknown, and one in my heart, trying to reconcile the growing distance back home.

Returning from Iraq as a commanding officer should have been one of the proudest moments of my life—a homecoming marked by celebration, relief, and reunion. When our plane touched down at Fort Sill, Oklahoma, after a year at war, I led my soldiers off the aircraft and into a gymnasium overflowing with signs, laughter, and families waiting with outstretched arms. I wore my uniform like armor, standing tall in my role, masking my own anticipation beneath rigid professionalism.

The room vibrated with emotion—I stood before my formation, took a breath, and called out the words I had waited months to say: "Soldiers, dismissed!"

In an instant, children sprinted to their parents, spouses collapsed into each other's arms, swallowed by hugs and celebration, tears fell like rain. I stood motionless, the only thing not moving in that sea of joy. My ex-wife, pregnant with our second child, was hundreds of miles away in New York. No family had come. No one was waiting.

I was surrounded by the sound of reunion—and I had no one to greet. The emptiness hit harder than anything I'd faced overseas.

One of my soldiers, seeing me standing alone, offered me a ride back to my house. I thanked him, holding back the ache in my chest. When I arrived, I had to knock on a neighbor's door just to get the spare key. I walked into that house alone—no lights on, furniture covered, air heavy with silence. The contrast between the roar of the gymnasium and the stillness of that empty house nearly buckled me. I had come home—but not really.

A week later, I flew to New York, finally holding my daughter for the first time in a year. She looked at me like I was a stranger—because to her, I was. I had missed her first steps, her first words, her beginning.

Before I could process that heartbreak, I was rushing to the hospital with my ex-wife for a high-risk pregnancy. My son was born just days later. I spent every hour by her side in that hospital room, doing everything I could to feel like I belonged to the life I had been away from for so long.

Only one person asked me the question I didn't even know I needed to hear: "Are you okay?"

It was her mother—not my soldiers, not the Army, not my family. She saw the man beneath the uniform. She somehow recognized what no one else had noticed: that in a matter of days, I had gone from leading men in combat, to walking into a homecoming with no one there, to sitting in a hospital chair trying to catch up on a life that had moved on without me.

No parades. No home-cooked meal. No space to breathe.

Just a hollow home, a distant child, and the weight of it all pressing down on my chest.

That was my reintroduction to a world that had moved forward while I had been frozen in war. That homecoming didn't feel like coming home. It felt like landing in a world I no longer belonged to. The isolation I felt planted the seeds of a truth I wouldn't understand until years later: you can be physically present and still completely absent. And that absence... was just beginning.

I didn't know how to come home. I had no roadmap for being vulnerable, for sharing, for connecting. Leadership in the army had taught me to sacrifice for others, but it hadn't taught me how to receive love or help. The truth is, I was in no place to be in a relationship, let alone a marriage.

I hadn't even begun the internal journey of self-awareness, healing, and emotional processing. I had no clue who was beneath my uniform, beneath that armor, beneath the discipline, beneath that responsibility.

So, how would I have ever been able to show up as a partner? I provided income and a roof over our heads, and I put food on the table, but I wasn't sure that I was capable of offering anything more than that. Intimacy, emotional presence, vulnerability—those were foreign languages to me. I thought being a good husband meant fulfilling my duties, not opening my heart.

Looking back now, I can see how much I expected of myself without understanding what I truly needed. I can also see how unfair it was to expect my ex-wife to reach someone who had no idea how to let himself be reached. As I said, leadership in the army had taught me to sacrifice for others, but not how to receive love or help.

A NEW MASK, SAME PAIN

I had traded one mask for another. The kid who had once smiled through trauma to avoid burdening his family, who had excelled in sports to avoid burdening his teammates, had become the soldier who smiled through war to avoid burdening his unit. I had mastered survival, but I still didn't know how to live.

What I didn't realize was that my strength had a cost, and one day, I would have to pay it. At West Point and in the Army, I knew who I was —cadet, athlete, leader, and officer. The uniform gave me a name, a purpose, a clear mission. But I never considered what would happen when the uniform came off. I didn't yet understand how much of my identity I had built on external structure. I mistook purpose for healing, and the day would come when the world no longer saluted and I'd have to face the question: Who am I without it all? Eventually, the structure of the military couldn't hold me together, and when I stepped into civilian life, the weight of everything I had buried came crashing down.

Sometimes, we chase belonging so desperately that we settle for places that reward our productivity but ignore our humanity. The military gave me discipline. It gave me routine and a mission. But it also gave me a new way to hide from the pain I wasn't ready to face.

KEY TAKEAWAYS FROM CHAPTER 2

- **Structure is not the same as healing** – Discipline can create stability, but it doesn't address emotional wounds if used as a way to avoid them.
- **Belonging without vulnerability isn't true connection** – You can be part of something bigger and still feel alone if you aren't seen for who you truly are beneath the role.
- **Performance is not purpose** – The world may reward what you *do*, but the deeper question is whether you *know* who you are without the title, uniform, or external validation.
- **Survival isn't the destination** – You can be highly successful on the outside and completely disconnected on the inside. True fulfillment requires more than endurance.

- **The cost of emotional disconnection is intimacy** – You cannot lead or love fully if you never learn how to receive support, show emotion, or be seen beyond your performance.

YOUR REFLECTION CHALLENGE

Pause and reflect on the ways you may have sought structure or status as a shield against deeper discomfort or pain:

1. Where in your life have you mistaken structure for healing?

   _____

   _____

   _____

2. What titles, roles, or identities have you clung to so you didn't have to face the harder questions beneath?

   _____

   _____

   _____

3. In what areas are you performing instead of being fully present?

_____

_____

_____

4. Have you ever built success on a foundation that silently cost you your peace, relationships, or health?

_____

_____

_____

5. What would it feel like to lead, love, or live without needing the mask of performance to feel worthy?

_____

_____

_____

You are not your rank, your role, or your resume.
You are worthy—without the uniform, without the title, without the applause.
The question now is... are you willing to meet yourself beneath it all?

CHAPTER 3
FROM BATTLEFIELD TO HOME FRONT: THE DUAL STRUGGLE

NAVIGATING LIFE BEYOND THE UNIFORM

When I came home from the military, I had everything I thought I wanted: a wife, children, a house with a yard, a new start.

However, my return wasn't just a change of address—it was emotional whiplash.

After my final deployment, my ex-wife told me she was moving back to Long Island with our children. "I can't live this military life anymore," she said.

Honestly, I didn't blame her. The military had taken me far away—physically and emotionally—for years. We decided it was best for the family.

I asked if we could compromise, find a place that gave me a shot at civilian transition while giving her a sense of stability. In the end, we went back to Long Island.

Returning home was more difficult than I imagined. I was surrounded by familiar faces who had never left, people who seemed stuck in time. It felt like I had journeyed across the world, fought wars, and now was back to square one, standing in the shadows of a past I'd tried to outrun. The return didn't feel like a homecoming. It felt like a trap.

I had broken free from my childhood circumstances. I was living the life I used to dream about—the one I thought would fix everything.

I had the opportunity to rewrite generational trauma and build something different, to protect my children, to raise them differently, to love them better. But the truth was—I still hadn't come home to myself.

I was brushing my kids' teeth at night, tucking them into bed, showing up to church, and bringing in the paycheck. But I wasn't really there. Not in a way that mattered.

My ex-wife had learned how to run the home without me during my deployments. She had her rhythm, her system, her independence.

I remember brushing our children's teeth one evening, trying to connect, trying to reclaim my role as a father, and she stepped in behind me and brushed them again, her way.

It seemed like such a small thing, but to me, it was a message written in capital letters: *"You're not needed here, not like you thought."*

We became two adults passing by one another in the same house. It was a quiet arrangement, emotionally muted, with each of us surviving in our own way.

I tried to step into the role of spiritual leader. I sat beside my family in church on Sundays. I stood for the hymns and bowed my head for the prayers. But I was still so far from myself.

I didn't know how to pray. I didn't know how to sit in silence. I didn't know how to listen for God's voice because I hadn't yet learned to listen for my own.

Still, I wanted faith for my children. I wanted them to feel rooted in something I never had.

So, I went. I showed up.

But showing up without presence is its own kind of absence. I was seeking God in a building, but I hadn't even begun to look for Him within.

FATHERHOOD IN THE FOG

This is where I must speak plainly—because this matters. At this time, I had three children, and I loved them with all my heart.

But love... isn't the same as presence.

I didn't know how to be home. I didn't know how to slow down, listen, sit still, or connect. I didn't know how to be a father outside of being a provider.

My routine became mechanical: up before they woke, out the door, home after bedtime.

Weekends were hit or miss—if I wasn't training or traveling for work, I was emotionally unavailable.

I was afraid to admit it, but it was true: I didn't know how to truly be with them. I didn't know how to open my heart when it had been armored shut for so long.

And they deserved more.

I wasn't intentionally neglectful. I was just... numb. And I didn't know how to come back online.

Looking back, I realize that the path to emotional presence doesn't begin with discipline—it begins with awareness. And I had none of it. This wasn't a failure of love. It was a failure of self-awareness. And that failure would shape what came next.

ADRENALINE, AVOIDANCE, AND THE CAGE

So, I did what I always did: I filled the void. Gambling became a fix. It gave me spikes, risks, rewards, and momentary highs that distracted me from the lows that I didn't even know how to face.

When gambling wasn't enough, I literally stepped into a cage. Cage fighting gave me purpose. The training, the grind, the intensity—it all mirrored the adrenaline I missed on the battlefield.

When you're fighting for something, even just for a win in the cage, it feels like control. It gave me purpose again.

Jiu-jitsu felt like my brotherhood. We didn't talk about feelings. We trained together. We bled together. We suffered together.

It felt familiar. Safe, in a twisted way. But deep down, I wasn't chasing the thrill; I was still running from stillness.

I wasn't ready to sit quietly. The noise was too loud. The memories were too close. I was trying to beat them back with adrenaline and avoidance.

I wasn't healing.

I was hiding.

So, I fought—with my fists and with fury.

NAVIGATING THE CORPORATE WORLD: A HARSH REALITY

Leaving the Army and stepping into corporate America was supposed to be my return to stability. Instead, it was the beginning of a different kind of war—a war within. For years, my identity had been defined by mission, rank, uniform, and urgency. My time had been owned by orders, objectives, and purpose.

Now, transitioning into civilian life, I found myself staring at a calendar full of blank spaces and a heart full of unanswered questions. The battlefield had changed, but the fight for identity and purpose had not.

Every day in combat, before we left the "wire" and after we returned, my soldiers and I would recite a powerful line: "Once more into the fray, into the last good fight I'll ever know. Live and die on this day. Live and die on this day."[1] It became a mantra, a way of life. Those words weren't

---

1. *The Grey*, directed by Joe Carnahan (2011).

just poetic—they were survival. They were how we made peace with every step forward.

Then, just like that, it was over.

There were no more morning formations, no mandatory PT, no missions to plan, no team to lead—just an open calendar and an empty house. I did my best to maintain structure, with 4:00 a.m. wake-ups, the gym, and work, but it was never enough. The silence, at first a relief, soon gave way to thoughts I had kept buried. But the quiet crept in.

And in the quiet came ghosts. Ghosts of war. Ghosts of childhood trauma. Ghosts of my father's absence—and my own looming fear of becoming just like him. I had become a West Point officer, a soldier. Without the uniform, without the battlefield, without the title... who was I? Without the uniform, I felt lost.

I took a job in the building materials industry. On paper, it was a great fit.

I brought leadership, experience, discipline, and a work ethic forged in fire, but nothing could have prepared me for how different it felt. Corporate life was very sterile. It was about margins, KPIs, and profit, not people.

In the Army, every mission had a team. You never ate alone. You trained, suffered, and overcame things together. But in my new life, I sat alone in a cubicle. I shook hands in boardrooms, but no one truly saw me. There were no fire teams, no brothers and sisters to my left and right, just polite small talk over coffee and a nameplate on a door.

I missed the unspoken bond, the looks that said, *I've got you.* In the civilian world, everyone was in their own silo, and I couldn't figure out how to belong. Leadership didn't mean mentorship or selfless service. It meant managing outputs and quarterly reviews.

In the military, when a soldier did a great job, I'd call him out in front of my formation and would present him with a certificate of appreciation. And it wasn't just a piece of paper. It was a moment of recognition.

It was a symbol of respect in front of your peers. The soldiers loved it. It lifted morale, created pride, and fueled the team.

I tried to carry that tradition into my new civilian role. One day, I called for a break and asked one of our top sales reps to stand in front of the room. To honor his efforts, I designed and printed a certificate of appreciation.

I gave a short speech praising his performance, and then I handed him the certificate with the same pride I would have used in uniform. He looked at me and then glanced around at the rest of the employees and said, "What is this? Can I cash it in at the bank? How about a gift card or a bonus?"

As the room erupted in laughter, the moment hit me like a brick. The shallowness, the entitlement, the disconnect—for the first time, I realized that I wasn't in the business of meaning anymore. I was in the business of metrics. There was no brotherhood or sisterhood. Where was the sacrifice for something bigger than yourself? I didn't just feel out of place; I felt lost.

This wasn't what I had thought service after service would look like.

WORK AS A NEW MASK: EARLY BURNOUT AND DISCONNECTION

So, I did what I always did: I performed myself. I overperformed. I arrived before sunrise. I outworked everyone. I chased every promotion, crushed every quota. And I was rewarded, praised, and promoted.

Work became my new addiction. It gave me something to focus on, somewhere to direct the chaos inside me. I smiled in meetings, crushed my quotas, and showed up relentlessly. This was another mask, another layer to an already thick armor. I wore my corporate title like a new uniform. Every raise and every new title felt like another layer of protection.

In truth, I was building a wall that no one, not even I, could see past.

I remember sitting in a meeting one day while people argued about a delayed shipment to a customer. Their voices were raised, and stress filled the room, but I felt nothing.

Just months before, I had been driving through an Iraqi village, navigating roads, trying to avoid roadside bombs, and now I was expected to panic over logistics and quarterly sales? My body was in the room, but my mind was elsewhere. I smiled. I nodded. I took notes. But inside, I felt like a ghost in a chair—hollow, unseen, unknown.

I was hiding in plain sight. I was hiding from my family, but most of all, I was hiding from myself. I was living a life that looked successful on the outside, but on the inside, I was lost, misaligned. My body was present, but my spirit was not.

The pattern was forming again: being rewarded for avoidance, searching for external validation, receiving praise for my pain. Underneath it all was the slow unraveling of a man who had no idea how to come home to himself.

THE HIDDEN WEIGHT OF PROFESSIONAL SUCCESS

In the civilian world, I brought the same relentless drive that I'd had my entire life and that I'd prided myself on in sports and the military. I didn't take days off. I didn't slow down. I took pride in that. Exhaustion was a badge of honor.

I believed that if I provided financially, I was doing enough. I believed that sacrificing rest made me a better man.

I was the first in and the last out. I beat every metric, hit every goal.

There were moments when the cracks showed—moments that no one saw. I remember how, while sitting in a meeting, the numbers on the screen blurred, the voices around me sounded distant, and my chest tightened. I smiled, nodded, and said something strategic. Then I excused myself, locked the bathroom door, and stared at my reflection, wondering how I'd gotten here. After a moment, I adjusted my collar, straightened my back, and returned to the meeting.

Another time, I snapped over a trivial situation with a customer. After hanging up the phone, I went into the employee kitchen and started pounding on the table with my fists. The frustration I felt wasn't due to the phone call. It was due to the pressure I had no outlet for. I apologized to any employees who'd heard my outburst, but the shame lingered.

One day, my regional manager sat me down and said, "You haven't taken a single day off in two and a half years." He mandated that I take a week off.

I argued. I told him I couldn't leave the team. Really, though, I couldn't leave the structure. I didn't know how to be still.

That staycation was anything but restful. I paced. I fidgeted. I counted down the days until I could return to my routine because, in the stillness, all the noise got louder.

I wasn't wired for peace. I was wired for pressure. I was wired for performance. I had mistaken busyness for purpose. I had also grown addicted to external validation—the high that came from being admired for how much I could carry.

Looking back now, I can see how desperately I needed someone to ask, not about what I did but how I was really doing. I needed someone to see the man behind the mask, but I hadn't even allowed myself to look.

My absence at home was obvious. But out in the world? I was praised.

And that made it easy to keep running.

THE FIFTH-GRADE CEREMONY: A WAKE-UP CALL

My daughter, now a high school senior, still brings it up: "Remember when you missed my fifth-grade graduation?"

She's said it gently over the years, but each time, it feels like a knife to the chest. Because she remembers.

She remembers the empty seat. She remembers that I wasn't there. She remembers my absence.

She remembers that I chose work.

No one at that company remembers that day. No one cared. But she did. And she still does.

That was the beginning of my realizing the truth: I was trading precious moments for hollow achievements.

RECOGNIZING THE SIGNS OF PTSD AND DEPRESSION

Over time, the very coping tools that helped me survive—discipline, drive, physicality—turned on me. They became obsessions. Work wasn't a career. It was camouflage.

What looked like success was actually overcompensation. Behind the controlled exterior were a mind and heart filled with unhealed trauma.

I hadn't dealt with the sexual abuse. I hadn't faced the physical beatings, the emotional abandonment, the fact that my father hadn't died of an aneurysm but by suicide, or the whispered stories of his death. And now the trauma from Iraq—the taking of lives, the weight of my men's safety, the ghosts I had brought home—was being layered on top.

The child who was never safe and the soldier who was never allowed to fall apart—they were now living inside the same exhausted body. The ghosts of my childhood were shaking hands with the ghosts of combat.

I was hypervigilant in every room. Crowds triggered me. Family events overwhelmed me. Holiday joy felt like pressure I couldn't rise to.

I sat at dinner with my family, physically present but light years away in my mind. I didn't laugh. I didn't play. I didn't know how to feel joy without guilt.

But at the gym? I was the big guy people liked to be around and asked for help.

And at work? I was sharp. Polished. Relentless. I was a corporate all-star.

I got promotions. Bonuses. Praise.

It all justified and validated my behavior. And it only deepened the illusion.

No one asked why I stayed late. No one questioned why I never took time off. Because high-functioning trauma looks a lot like excellence—until it doesn't.

The more praise I received, the more disconnected I became from the people who mattered most. It validated my absence at home. It rewarded my pain. I didn't know how to feel, and the one thing that helped me feel something was applause from people who didn't know the real me.

The walls were just beginning to crack. What I didn't know was that the breaking point was closer than I thought.

THE GROWING DIVIDE IN MY FAMILY LIFE

The gap in my marriage grew wider by the day.

During the turbulent times of my marriage, I often believed that relocating from New York to North Carolina would be the solution to our problems. I argued that we could pioneer the move for our family, believing a new environment would fix everything. My ex-wife, in her wisdom, would always challenge this notion, reminding me that running away wouldn't solve our issues.

Looking back, I see the truth in her words. Healing and growth come from within, not from changing locations. It's not about altering what we see but how we see it, but I was nowhere near ready to understand or embrace this yet.

I knew something was wrong, but I didn't have the emotional capacity or tools to fix it or face it.

So I did what I knew how to do: I controlled my schedule. I built my body. I chased professional wins.

All the while, I was quietly unraveling.

On the outside, I had it all: a beautiful family, a great job, and a nice home. On the inside, I was walking around with a pain I didn't have words for.

At my ex-wife's encouragement, I finally sought help through the VA. After one session, I was diagnosed with PTSD and depression and sent home with a prescription for Lexapro.

It numbed me even further. Now I didn't just feel detached—I felt like a ghost.

I wasn't healing; I was sedated, and the craving for external validation only grew louder. I needed someone, somewhere, to tell me I was okay— because I couldn't tell myself.

And all the while, I was slipping further from the people I loved.

No one teaches you how to go from combat zones to conference rooms. No one prepares you for what it means to take a life in the name of honor, only to later witness the miracle of life and not know how to feel it, how to hold it, how to connect to it, or how to realize that your soul can't catch up to either.

I was chasing belonging in all the wrong places, settling for environments that praised my output but ignored my soul.

Maybe you've done the same. Maybe you've buried yourself in work, distractions, or achievement, not realizing what you were trying to outrun.

But here's the truth: you can't outrun yourself. Eventually, the pain catches up.

And when it does... you get to decide what happens next.

The walls were cracking. My mask was slipping, and the weight I carried—the childhood pain, the combat trauma, the pressure to provide, the fear of failure—was building toward collapse. What no one saw was that I didn't just feel like I was drowning. I was about to go under.

KEY TAKEAWAYS FROM CHAPTER 3

1. **You can be surrounded by people and still feel completely alone.**
2. Belonging isn't about where you live or what you do—it's about who you *are* when no one is watching.
3. **Numbing isn't healing.**
4. Whether it's through work, adrenaline, addiction, or avoidance—distraction may quiet the noise temporarily, but it will never bring true peace.
5. **Success on the outside doesn't heal emptiness on the inside.**
6. You can be praised for your performance and still be crumbling privately. The world may reward your mask, but your soul knows the truth.
7. **Presence is not about being there physically; it's about being there *fully*.**
8. Love requires more than showing up. It requires vulnerability, awareness, and connection.
9. **You cannot fix internal pain with external achievements.**
10. A new job, a new city, a new title, or a new distraction will never replace the deep work of facing yourself.
11. **Avoidance breeds deeper disconnection.**
12. What you don't face will control you—until you choose to turn toward it with courage and honesty.
13. **There is no perfect environment for healing—only the brave decision to begin.**

14. Healing isn't about where you go next. It's about who you are willing to become, right where you are.

YOUR REFLECTION CHALLENGE

1. Where in your life are you *physically present* but *emotionally absent*? Who is waiting for you to show up—not just with your body, but with your heart?

_____

_____

_____

2. What are you distracting yourself with right now to avoid feeling what's really going on inside? Is it work? Fitness? Social media? Busyness? What are you afraid might surface if you stop?

_____

_____

_____

3. When was the last time you *truly* listened to yourself—not your title, not your to-do list, but your *soul*? What is it trying to tell you that you've been too busy or too scared to hear?

_____

_____

_____

4. Have you ever mistaken *achievement* for *healing*? What "success" have you chased that was really just a way to feel worthy?

_____

_____

_____

5. What would it look like to let go of the mask you wear for the world? Who would benefit if you showed up *fully human*, not *perfectly polished*?

_____

_____

_____

6. Are you hoping the next promotion, relationship, or environment will fix what feels broken inside? What would change if you stopped *running toward the next thing* and started *turning toward yourself*?

_____

_____

_____

7. What pain have you been avoiding that needs your attention —not to punish you, but to free you?

_____

_____

_____

You don't have to wait for a collapse to make a change. You can choose to reconnect now. To slow down. To listen. Because your family doesn't need your perfection. They need your presence.

CHAPTER 4
THE BREAKING POINT

THE ILLUSION OF SUCCESS WHILE DROWNING INTERNALLY

From the outside looking in, it all looked like winning: promotions, praise, paychecks. I was the high-performing professional, the leader who always showed up. But behind the scenes, I was crumbling.

The very system that praised me was also feeding the darkest parts of me. My trauma-driven behavior—overworking, never resting, sacrificing sleep—was seen as excellence. But it wasn't noble. It was avoidance, and it was slowly killing me. The numbness wasn't new, but this time, it felt complete, like even my body had stopped pretending. I was hollowed out. There was no fight left, just quiet. And it was too quiet.

I had mastered the art of hiding in plain sight. My schedule was so tightly packed that it left me no room to feel, no room to breathe, no room for the truth, no room for self-awareness, and no room for self-love.

RUNNING ON EMPTY: THE UNSEEN COLLAPSE

The VA and its team of psychiatrists accomplished the mission. I was not battling as many highs and lows. I was not as hypervigilant. I was actually nothing at all, completely sedated on their antidepressants, and every time I told them that I was numb to life, with absolutely no drive emotionally, physically, or intimately, all they did was change the dosage or add different medications.

My ex-wife was officially declared my "caregiver" by the VA. This meant that she maintained physical control over any and all prescription bottles and would monitor me taking the medication. This is what it had come to.

I felt nothing anymore. I had no purpose. I had no way of understanding how I could be looked at as such a success in the eyes of others, often given the nickname "Captain America," yet internally having no identity, self-dignity, or self-worth. I wasn't even allowed to take my own medicine.

WHAT THE MILITARY DOES NOT TRAIN YOU FOR

The Army trains you to endure, to protect, to lead, but it doesn't train you to grieve. It doesn't prepare you for the silence after the gunfire stops. It doesn't prepare you to carry the lives you couldn't save. It doesn't train you to ask for help, and it doesn't train you to release control. So, after the military, when all this starts to surface, you have the VA.

The VA's answer? "Here's Lexapro."

No questions. No real help. Just sedation.

The medication numbed me until I felt even less than before. My trauma wasn't being treated. It was being buried deeper.

FORGED IN ARMOR, FREED BY LOVE

THE SUICIDE ATTEMPT AND THE 72-HOUR EVALUATION

That day is seared into my memory.

Before anything else, I had to spend time with my children. I ran a bath for each of them. I washed them gently, slowly, not rushing like usual, not distracted, soaking in the weight of what I knew I was about to do. I kissed their foreheads and held them longer than usual. I looked them in the eyes, really looked, until it hurt to look any longer, and in my heart, I said goodbye.

Then I walked outside and across the lawn of our house at the end of a dead-end street. Each blade of grass felt like a tether trying to hold me to the earth. I dragged my feet as if to leave a mark behind. And then I stopped.

Right in the middle of the road.

I looked up at the sky.

"Dad," I said, my voice cracking under the weight of every unsaid word, "I get it. I can't do this anymore. I don't want to be here."

And for the first time in my life, I truly understood him.

The man I had judged. The man I had resented. The man I had grieved but never forgiven.

I finally saw what he had seen. Felt what he must have felt. The unbearable noise. The silent war in the mind. The weight of pain that love, even the deepest love, couldn't carry away.

No one had ever loved their children more than I did, but even that love couldn't save me from myself anymore.

I created a plan and set it in motion. I chose a hotel far enough from my family that they wouldn't find me. I thought I was doing them a favor. I reserved the room for one night, and I drove myself there like I was checking into a business trip.

The room was cold. Dimly lit.

I opened a bottle of alcohol and reached for the bottle of antidepres-

45

sants I had taken from the cabinet at home. Then I sat there in that room of muted colors and buzzing silence. The thoughts in my head had finally gone still. Not peace, exactly, but a kind of quiet I hadn't known in years.

How? How had it all come to this?

I sat in that chair, staring at the wall, thinking it would all be over soon. Somehow, that thought brought a strange sense of comfort.

But my ex-wife knew. She had seen it in me that day and knew something was off.

She called the police and told them she feared for my safety. When they pinged my phone, they found the hotel.

Four officers arrived at my door. One carried authority. She spoke like I was a threat.

But two of them, two combat veterans, saw me. Not the broken man in front of them but the man I had been. A fellow soldier. A fellow fighter.

"Treat him with care," they begged their supervisor. "He's one of us." But their voices were overruled.

They handcuffed me, the high school hall-of-famer, the West Point graduate, the military officer, the corporate success story. Now I was sitting in a hotel room with my wrists bound.

My head hung in shame as they marched me out through the front lobby, and when I looked up, I saw them: my older and younger brothers, standing in the lobby, their eyes wet with tears. Their presence broke me, but it also held me.

I was taken to a psychiatric facility and placed on a 72-hour hold. I had gone from being "Captain America" to a psych ward, from the one everyone leaned on to the one who couldn't take another step.

THE AFTERMATH

Couples therapy. Marriage counseling. Religious weekend retreats. My ex-wife and I tried everything. Neither of us wanted to break up our family through divorce, but we had no other path. After packing a bag of clothes, I moved into the basement apartment of one of my friends. My ex-wife and I tried to mask our separation from our children. My schedule had me gone before they woke and home after they were asleep. For a while, they didn't even notice, and I was ok with that because I couldn't convince myself that I brought any value to them as a father.

But the weight of pretending and the grief of unraveling caught up with me. For months, I wasn't just absent physically—I was emotionally unreachable. Sitting in that basement apartment, surrounded by nothing but silence—and the silence was deafening.

To the Reader: When the darkness didn't take me, I was left with one question echoing in the silence: *Now what?* What came next wasn't healing—not yet—but the slow, painful decision to begin choosing life, one breath, one moment at a time.

Maybe you've had a breaking point, too, that moment when you feel like you've done everything right, but it still wasn't enough, when even the love you have for your family feels like it's not enough to hold you here.

Let me tell you, that moment is not the end.

It's the moment where you get to choose what comes next.

Pain doesn't get the final say. *You do.*

When the darkness didn't take me, I was left with one question echoing in the silence: *Now what?* What came next wasn't healing—not yet—but the slow, painful decision to begin choosing life, one breath, one moment at a time.

KEY TAKEAWAYS FROM CHAPTER 4

- **Success is not immunity from suffering** – You can wear the mask of high performance and still be silently drowning.
- **Numbing isn't healing** – Sedation is not the same as restoration. True healing begins when you stop avoiding and start facing.
- **There's nothing noble about burning out** – Sacrificing your well-being in the name of "providing" or performing only deepens the pain.
- **Suicide is not selfish—it's a silence misunderstood** – Understanding doesn't condone, but it creates space for compassion—for yourself and for those who have been lost.
- **Your breaking point is not your end—it's your turning point** – The moment when the pain becomes unbearable is also the moment when you're invited to begin again.

YOUR REFLECTION CHALLENGE

This chapter asks you to pause and sit with some of life's hardest questions—not to judge yourself, but to begin reclaiming your story:

1. What parts of yourself have you sacrificed to maintain the illusion of success?

_____

_____

_____

2. Are you using busyness, overachievement, or distraction to avoid deeper pain?

_____

_____

_____

3. What would it mean to admit you're not okay—and that be okay?

_____

_____

_____

4. Have you reached a breaking point and convinced yourself it's the end, when it may be the beginning?

_____

_____

_____

5. Who or what would you need to feel truly supported in your healing journey?

_____

_____

_____

Your worth was never tied to your achievements.
And your life is not over because it hurts right now.
There is life after the breakdown.
And it just might be the most honest, beautiful version of life
you've ever lived.

CHAPTER 5
CHOOSING TO FIGHT FOR MY LIFE

THE MOMENT EVERYTHING CLICKED

That moment in the street, looking up at the sky, speaking to my father, shattered something in me—but it also cracked something open.

For the first time, I acknowledged his death. For the first time, I let myself feel him. And for the first time, I spoke to him.

I had never talked about him growing up. Never asked questions. I had frozen myself on the day I learned the truth—that his "aneurysm" was a lie, and his death had been a suicide.

But standing there, I let the truth in. I let the grief hit me. And it hurt like hell. It cut deep.

Strangely, it was also quietly peaceful.

Not hope. Not healing. Not yet. But clarity.

Between the father who couldn't stay and the son who finally understood, something shifted. It was the beginning of feeling again.

I didn't reclaim my power that day. I didn't transform. But I woke up.

I named the pain. I faced it. And that started to change everything.

There was still so much work ahead—layers to peel back, armor to chip away. But for the first time, I had faced what I had spent a lifetime running from. And that changed everything.

THE 72-HOUR WAKE-UP CALL

Those three days in the psych facility were some of the longest, quietest, and most brutal hours of my life.

No rank, no medals, no uniform, just hospital scrubs and silence. I wasn't an athlete. I wasn't a captain. I wasn't a business leader.

I was just another man trying to make it through each hour, each day. The walls of that room didn't just keep me in; they kept everything else out.

I stared at myself in the mirror, and I saw a man I didn't recognize. For the first time, though, I didn't look away. I forced myself to keep looking.

The voices in my head were loud, filled with regret, shame, embarrassment, failure, and fear, but in the middle of all that noise, something new emerged, a new thought: *This is not the end.*

A WARRIOR WITHIN: CHOOSING TO FIGHT

After my 72-hour hold, I stepped out into the world with something new, an ember, a spark of life. I wasn't healed, and I wasn't whole, but I was awake, barely. For the first time, I was willing to try.

Everything in me wanted to rebuild. I leaned on what I knew best: the warrior inside me. All my life, I had been trained to fight. My childhood, sports, West Point, combat, cage fighting, hustling in the corporate world. I knew how to push. I knew how to endure. I knew how to win.

All those years of discipline, resilience, and pushing through pain had

FORGED IN ARMOR, FREED BY LOVE

helped me survive the darkness. Maybe those same tools could now help me walk toward light. Maybe they could finally help me fight for myself.

Healing isn't soft; healing is war, and I was done being a prisoner of my mind. I didn't know how to heal yet, but I did know how to fight.

So, I started there. What I didn't realize was that even in the season of healing, I was still trying to control the process, still trying to fix from the outside what could only be healed from within.

THE RELATIONSHIP THAT WASN'T WHAT I THOUGHT

Around this time, I entered a new relationship. I truly believed this would be the answer. She brought light into my life, comfort, and a sense of purpose.

I thought I was finally happy. I was doing better. I wanted to live.

I was being more present. I believed that this was my transformation, but beneath the surface, something else was happening. I didn't realize that I had attached my entire identity, my happiness, my sense of self-worth to her. My mood rose and fell with her responses.

Years later, I would learn about codependency and relationship styles. I mistook codependency for connection and validation for love. Everything I had dealt with, the trauma, the insecurity, the lack of self-worth, it was all still very much there. It was just redirected to another person.

She became my emotional lifeline, not because she asked to be, but because I didn't know how to anchor myself. I've always thought of myself as a lover. I give all of myself to the people I care about, but this time, I began to see the truth.

I was giving 100 percent of myself to someone else because I had no idea how to give even ten percent to me.

When I separated from my ex-wife, I packed a single bag and moved into a friend's basement. Over the next few years, I transitioned through multiple basement apartments, financially strained but determined to provide for my children. Despite the hardships, my unwavering effort in my corporate career allowed me to secure a second mortgage and buy a home. I transformed my house, adding a pool and creating a beautiful space for my kids, who had only known the instability of basement living.

Once I completed the renovations to make it feel like a true home for my children—who stayed with me every weekend—I felt a deep sense of accomplishment. But then I noticed something. That house only felt like a home from Friday night through Sunday night, when my kids were there. The moment they packed their bags and left on Sunday evenings, the walls seemed to close in around me.

The house I had worked so hard to buy and rebuild became a reminder of everything I believed I had failed at, especially the vows I had made to myself as a child to one day create a family rooted in protection and unconditional love.

I couldn't yet see that I was providing that love, just in a different way. All I saw was emptiness.

So, I fought for a promotion. Why? Because I still had no self-awareness. I didn't have the tools yet to understand the complexities of the mind. And when I earned that promotion, it felt like the solution. It covered four states and required constant travel. My kids would leave for their mom's house on Sunday nights, and so would I—off to whatever hotel was booked in whatever state I was working in that week. My deal with the company was simple: I didn't care where I had to go, as long as I was back by 5:00 p.m. every Friday to greet my kids when they returned.

The perfect distraction. More professional success. More praise. More validation

From the outside, it seemed like I was thriving yet again, as I was rebuilding, achieving, and excelling in my career. However, this external success came with a price. The praise and affirmation from my company became a crutch, a space where I lost myself, still unaware of the inner work I needed to do to break free from the need for external validation.

The journey of rebuilding the home for my children showed them resilience—that no matter what, we can rise and rebuild. But as the walls of our new home stood tall, my inner struggles remained. The codependent relationship I was in began to crumble, as she could see how important others' recognition and admiration were to me, especially in moments when she could not give me the attention I needed.

WHEN IT FELL APART, SO DID I

Eventually, the crack showed my neediness, my over-reliance, my constant scanning for rejection. She left, and I spiraled.

It wasn't just heartbreak; it was devastation. I fell into a depression again, one that felt just as dark as before. I didn't understand how I could be back there again.

Then something clicked. I realized that the pain I was feeling had almost nothing to do with her. What I was mourning was the collapse of the illusion that someone else could be my oxygen, my purpose, my salvation.

This was the moment I finally understood how deeply I had tied my worth to external validation from my childhood, to the military, to work, to public praise, and now to love. This was the moment I knew that I had never truly loved myself.

Until I did, no one else's love would ever be enough.

THE SECOND 72-HOUR WAKE-UP CALL

That breakup was my second wake-up call. Unlike with the psych facility, no one came to rescue me. So, I would have to rescue myself.

The realization was sobering. I was still operating from the same patterns, just with a new packaging.

The suit was different, but the storyline had not changed. The pain underneath was the same. I was still fighting for worth, still outsourcing my peace, still trying to earn love instead of receiving it.

CHOOSING REAL RESILIENCE

This time, the decision to rebuild came from a deeper place. I said to myself, *No more looking outward first. It's time to go inward.*

I had to learn what self-love looked like, not just as a concept but as a discipline, a practice, a belief. It wasn't flashy. It wasn't dramatic.

It looked like waking up early to breathe, saying "no" to things that drained me, and being kind to myself on days that I didn't perform. I had to treat myself like someone worth loving before expecting anyone else to. There was no lightning-bolt moment, no sudden epiphany, just a quiet decision whispered from somewhere deep inside.

No more, no more hiding, no more pretending, no more running. I didn't want to just survive anymore. I wanted to rebuild.

I wanted to live. I wanted to love myself. Acknowledging my pain didn't make me weak. It made me real.

And for the first time, I gave myself permission to be both wounded and worthy. I stopped defining myself by what broke me and started imagining who I could become.

THE OVERTIME MENTALITY

In sports, when regulation ends in a tie, you enter overtime. It's where games are no longer won by talent alone—it's where they're won by heart.

I had entered the overtime of my life. This wasn't about going back to who I used to be. That version of me was gone.

This was about fighting forward—with heart, with humility, with grit.

Healing had become my new mission.

It required endurance, strategy, and showing up every day, even on the days I didn't want to. Especially on those days.

Overtime doesn't care about the scoreboard. It cares about how much heart you bring when the game's on the line.

This wasn't just overtime in my survival story. This was the overtime of my awakening.

It was here that I began planting seeds for a new life—one rooted in intention and truth.

As I sat in the silence I had spent years avoiding, I started to see the cost of my old choices—missed milestones. Emotional distance. Strained relationships. The slow erosion of my own sense of self.

I was done chasing validation.

I was choosing peace.

Buried beneath the layers of titles, roles, and expectations, I started to see a new way forward.

I made a vow:

No more sacrificing the people I love for performance.
No more trading peace for applause.
No more building a life that looked good on the outside but felt empty on the inside.

Instead, I would build something real—

A life of alignment, not just of appearance.

That vow planted the first seeds of what would one day become my healing work, my business, and my redefined leadership. I began to understand that healing wasn't just about fighting pain. It was about making room for joy, self-compassion, and wholeness.

That seed would soon grow into coaching, community, the Warrior Ranch, and eventually, the life-altering experiences that awaited me in the mountains of Mexico.

But first, I had to stop outsourcing my identity.

I had to come home to myself.

Maybe you have felt like your life was finally on track until it wasn't. Maybe you thought you found the thing that you would fix. Maybe you thought you found the thing that would fix you, a job, a relationship, a status, but then it all collapsed. Now you're left wondering, *Was any of it real? Was any of it mine?*

I want to tell you, the collapse is a gift. It strips away all the illusion. Now you get to build something real, not around someone else, but around you.

You don't need to be perfect. You just need to be willing to keep showing up every day with intention. What part of your story do you need to reclaim? What pain are you allowing to define your identity today? What would happen if you chose to fight, not for survival but for peace? Who are you when there's no one left to impress? Are you ready to stop abandoning yourself in the name of keeping others happy? What would change if you gave yourself the same love and devotion you give to everyone else?

As I began to rebuild, as I began to turn inward, I started to ask new questions. I needed a connection. I needed purpose. I needed something that reminded me of who I was before the armor. So, I returned to the field, to coaching, to connection, to community.

And that started the change.

KEY TAKEAWAYS FROM CHAPTER 5

- **Healing begins when you stop outsourcing your worth to others** – No job, relationship, or achievement can give you what only you can give yourself: inner peace.
- **You can rebuild—but real rebuilding starts within** – Physical success without emotional alignment will always feel hollow.

- **Codependency is not connection** – True love is rooted in wholeness, not in needing someone else to complete you.
- **The real fight isn't for status—it's for inner freedom** – Overtime in life isn't about pushing harder; it's about softening, awakening, and choosing peace.
- **Every collapse reveals a new choice** – The fall isn't the end —it's the clearing for something more authentic to grow.

YOUR REFLECTION CHALLENGE

This chapter invites you to stop chasing outside fixes and start asking deeper questions:

1. Where in your life are you looking to someone or something else to give you worth?

_____

_____

_____

2. Have you mistaken busyness or productivity for healing?

_____

_____

_____

3. What illusion are you holding on to that is keeping you from building something real?

_____

_____

_____

4. What would it look like to create peace within yourself—not after you "achieve" something, but right now, exactly as you are?

_____

_____

_____

5. Are you willing to fight—not to prove yourself—but to come home to yourself?

_____

_____

_____

You don't need to wait for another breakdown to begin again.
You can stop running. You can choose peace.
Your new life begins the moment you decide to stop abandoning yourself.

CHAPTER 6
REBUILDING THROUGH CONNECTION, SPORTS, SERVICE, AND SHOWING UP

COACHING AS A PATH TO RECONNECTION

My journey back to presence didn't begin in a therapist's chair or at a retreat, although those are also parts of my story. It began in a gymnasium at my daughter's first lacrosse practice. I showed up to that practice wearing an old Army Lacrosse sweatshirt from my days at West Point.

I wasn't expecting anything more than just being a parent or a spectator on the sidelines, but the director of the program, Jen, came up to me with wide eyes and excitement. "You played at West Point? You played for Army?" she asked.

"Yeah," I said with a chuckle, thinking back to my glory days.

"Then you have to coach your daughter's team."

I laughed again, nervously this time. "Uh, I don't think you want an Army combat veteran and a former Army D1 lacrosse player coaching little girls. And I know nothing about the girls' game, as it varies greatly from the boys."

But Jen persisted, and thank God that she did. That moment led to one of the most rewarding experiences of my life.

Eleven years later, I'm still coaching girls lacrosse, not just for my daughters but for dozens of other young athletes who have become like family to me. Stepping onto the field in a new role began to heal something between me and my children.

It wasn't about the game. It wasn't about athletics. It was about time. It was about presence. It was about connection.

Coaching became the bridge between me and my children, an emotional repair that I didn't even know we needed. Weekend tournaments, long road trips, sidewalk conversations, car rides full of conversation, laughter, music, reflection, talks about school, friends, relationships.

I began leading with love, not with strategy; coaching them to win in life, not just on the athletic field or in games. For the first time in a long time, I was showing up emotionally as well as physically.

They felt it. I felt it. And that shift was undeniable.

THE POWER OF BEING ON A TEAM AGAIN

There's something sacred about being a part of a team.

I had missed it more than I had realized. Coaching rekindled my understanding of what it means to trust, mentor, and build something together. It was no longer about chasing trophies. It was about creating belonging. This was leadership, not performance-based, but people-centered. I was learning to lead without force, to guide with presence, to influence with consistency and care, not control.

The sideline became my new battlefield. But this time, the mission was love, and the wins looked like smiles, confidence, resilience, and trust. It was an amazing opportunity to remember just how powerful we are together as people.

One thing I used to ask my soldiers all the time, and what I now ask my children, employees, and coworkers, is what is the military's greatest resource? I would get answers like "our tanks," "our planes," and "our weapons," and I would say, "No, you are. Without people, none of it matters." I've transitioned that into all my conversations, and I've challenged my children with it in coaching and life as a reminder that it's not about performance but about being people-centered.

SHOOTOUT FOR SOLDIERS, THE VETERAN COMMUNITY, AND WEST POINT ALUMNI

My friend Erik runs Shootout for Soldiers, a 24-hour lacrosse event raising awareness and support for veterans. For years, he always told me to stay involved with the community and with veterans. He preaches about the strength in this.

Eventually, I listened. For the first time, I laced up my cleats and joined other veterans on the field.

When I did, I felt something I hadn't felt in years: camaraderie, connection, the brotherhood and sisterhood that I thought was gone. I've now been a part of that event for ten consecutive years.

The same thing happened when I returned to West Point for an alumni lacrosse weekend and game. Graduating from the military academy was one of the most challenging yet proudest milestones of my life. When I left, I vowed never to return, determined that the last image of West Point would be in my rearview mirror driving off the grounds after graduation.

Memories were rewarding, however, they were also heavy—laden with pressure and pain. They reminded me of the agony of being stripped of the title of team captain. They reminded me of the unfulfillment of missing my class' graduation ceremony. The sting of those experiences, and many others, made me vow never to return—until years later, when I finally did.

And when I did return for an alumni weekend and game, the floodgates opened: emotion, pride, healing. Putting that jersey back on didn't just take me back; it felt like it brought me home. I finally allowed myself to be proud of the warrior I had become, not just the battles I had fought and lost.

The moment I jogged onto the field, something familiar and sacred returned. Just like in high school, just like at West Point, I felt it. I felt the dew on the grass hitting my cleats. I felt the warmth of the sun as it touched my skin, the wind as it whistled through my helmet.

As I locked my eyes on the American flag during the national anthem, I felt tears well up. Back in my competitive days, I always had a strange duality in me. I could feel nature's details with reverence and then snap into game mode with complete mental readiness. I never understood what that meant, but I noticed it. I felt it. It was all divine, but I never asked why I noticed it.

Now I was here, older, slower, and not here to win but to belong. I still noticed it all, but this time, I didn't have to analyze or compete. I didn't have to worry about the strategy of the game.

I just absorbed it. I felt it. And for the first time, I realized that those moments of presence were never about strategy. They were spiritual. They were sacred.

I didn't know it yet, not fully, but something inside of me was stirring. I was being called back, back to stillness, back to awareness, back to nature, and most importantly, back to myself.

THE HIDDEN TRANSFORMATION BEHIND THE JERSEY

Joining the alumni group of West Point Lacrosse players was a profound step in my healing journey. Coaching lacrosse, playing for Shootout for Soldiers, and attending alumni weekends and games reconnected me deeply with the values of community and brotherhood. It awakened an awareness of how these connections were vital to my recovery.

A transformative program started by the head Army lacrosse coach further deepened this bond. The initiative connected every current player with all former players who had worn the same jersey number. For me, this meant receiving an email from Danny Kielbasa, the current bearer of number 23. He introduced himself and shared his story, and soon, we exchanged phone numbers. What started as a simple email evolved into a long-distance friendship filled with texts before and after games, weekly check-ins, and mutual support.

This program wasn't just about maintaining the legacy; it was about fostering a living, breathing community that extended beyond the field. It reconnected me to a brotherhood and reminded me that I was still a part of something greater. My friendship with Danny and his willingness to create this relationship with an older alumnus are testaments to the power of this connection, reflecting the deeper healing and recovery that comes from being a part of a community and legacy.

Wearing that jersey again, whether for a youth team, an alumni game, or a veterans event, was never just about the sport. It was about reclaiming myself. Sports became the bridge from isolation to inclusion, from performance to presence, from armor to authenticity.

Fighting in a cage was about survival; it was about me. Coaching on the sidelines was about selfless service to others. That shift taught me something powerful.

I didn't need to perform to be valuable. I just needed to show up with love, consistency, and heart. Healing doesn't have to be lonely, and being a part of something bigger than yourself can reignite your purpose in ways that solitude never could.

LAYING THE FOUNDATION FOR LEADERSHIP AND BUSINESS

What I was learning through coaching began to ripple into my professional life.

Patience, emotional intelligence, servant leadership, and presence. I started building my business around these values, not just to succeed but to lead in ways that were aligned with my healing. I realized that I didn't want to just be any leader.

I wanted to be the leader I always needed, the kind who sees people, who shows up, who leads with love, not just strategy. Success was no longer defined by metrics. It was defined by impact.

You don't have to be a coach to show up for the people in your life. Sometimes, healing looks like passing a ball, driving a teammate to practice, or cheering from the sidelines. You do not need to be perfect. You just need to be present.

When was the last time you were a part of something bigger than yourself? Are you showing up for the people you love? Or are you just present in body but absent in spirit and mind? What would it look like for you to lead with love instead of performance? What hidden gifts are waiting to emerge when you stop trying to prove something and start trying to connect?

Coaching brought me back to community, but something deeper still called to me, something more intuitive, more ancient, more connected to nature and energy. I had no idea that my next breakthrough wouldn't come with a jersey or a game. It would come from a silent, four-legged teacher named Fiona.

KEY TAKEAWAYS FROM CHAPTER 6

- **Healing can happen in relationships, not just isolation** – The most powerful breakthroughs often come when we show up for others, not just ourselves.
- **You don't have to wear a uniform to belong** – True community isn't earned through achievement; it's found in connection, consistency, and presence.
- **You are your family's greatest resource** – Your children, your team, your community—they don't need your perfection; they need *you*.
- **Service isn't about sacrifice alone—it's about showing up with heart** – You don't need to fight for validation when you realize you already belong.
- **True fulfillment is built in the small moments** – The way you show up today is already shaping the future of those around you.

YOUR REFLECTION CHALLENGE

Pause for a moment and reflect on these questions:

1. Where in your life have you mistaken performance for connection?

_____

_____

_____

2. Who needs you to show up, not perfectly, but presently?

_____

_____

_____

3. When was the last time you felt part of something bigger than yourself?

_____

_____

_____

4. What would change if you stopped trying to prove your worth—and started leading with love?

_____

_____

_____

5. What's one small way you can reconnect with your family, your team, or your community this week?

_____

_____

_____

CHAPTER 7

THE LESSONS OF THE HORSE: HEALING THROUGH EQUINE THERAPY

FIRST ENCOUNTER: A SEED IS PLANTED

Years before I ever began this healing journey, before I had the words to name what I was searching for, I met a horse named Fiona.

At that time, my ex-wife wanted to take our kids on a family vacation to a dude ranch in upstate New York, a place she had gone with her family growing up. It was packed with daily activities, campfires, line dancing, rodeos, and horse trail rides. But what I remember most was Fiona.

Fiona was a massive horse, beautiful and powerful. I felt like I saw myself in her in a way that I didn't understand.

She wasn't being used for the trail rides. Instead, she was being kept in a stall, seemingly just observing this world with deep, calm eyes. I found myself gravitating toward her every day. I never spoke to her. I never pet her. I just stood there and watched her.

The horse trainer noticed and asked if I wanted to come closer. Eventually, he let me ride Fiona. Something about just being near her soothed me.

I couldn't explain it at the time. I wouldn't have known how. I didn't even understand it at that time.

But it stayed with me. That moment with Fiona stirred something in me: a quiet knowing that this space, this energy, this presence had meaning.

I wasn't ready then, but the seed had been planted.

SEEKING MORE: FINDING THE WARRIOR RANCH

At the end of the codependent relationship that I once thought was my transformation, I could feel the darkness creeping back in. This time, however, I had something I didn't have before: awareness. Not total healing, not self-love yet, but awareness—enough to know that I couldn't go backward.

I would not go backward. I had my rituals, Shootout for Soldiers, and my West Point alumni weekends, but they were occasional. I needed something more. Something more consistent. Something grounding.

Then, like a gift from the universe, I remembered Fiona and that moment at the dude ranch almost a decade prior. I opened my laptop and typed into Google, "veterans, horses, Long Island." I just felt like something had to exist.

The first search result was Warrior Ranch in Calverton, New York, just 25 minutes from where I lived. I filled out the contact form on the website. Within an hour, I got a call from Juliette, the lead coordinator, who, today, is one of my best friends.

She explained the program, the ranch's mission, and the vision of Eileen, the president of Warrior Ranch. A nonprofit born in Eileen's kitchen, it was dedicated to pairing veterans and first responders with rescue horses for mutual healing—America's heroes rescuing America's icons. I was in. Juliette gave me the date for their next retreat, and I booked it immediately.

I arrived with no idea of what to expect. I was anxious, curious, and hopeful. The first retreat changed me.

I was paired with Cody, the ranch president's horse, for the morning session. Cody was calm, responsive, and well-trained. Afterward, when I went to lunch, I felt like I was born to do this, a natural horseman.

Then the afternoon came—enter Schmay, the mini. I laughed when they paired me with him, thinking, *This will be so easy compared to the first half of the day.* Well, Schmay kicked my ego's ass. He didn't listen. He pushed back. He showed me that this wasn't about size or control. It was about energy, presence, and humility.

In that space, with the wind, trees, and beauty of the environment, I found something I hadn't even known I was missing: stillness, peace, and real presence.

HOW HORSES REFLECT OUR ENERGY

Horses don't speak. They feel. They don't care what you've done, what your title is, what rank you are, or what you're trying to prove.

They mirror your energy with exactness. They will actually sync their heartbeats to yours. If you're anxious, they'll be anxious. If you're grounded, they will follow you anywhere. Horses have no agenda. They simply respond to who you are in that moment, not who you pretend to be.

One day, I was training with Joe and James from Slick Horns Horsemanship. We were working on team roping, and I was frustrated. I could not get it right. George, the roping horse, kept fighting me. He wasn't listening. I was trying to force it. I kept trying to control everything.

James pulled me aside. "Take a break," he said.

I walked away, defeated, frustrated, and found a corner of the pen. There, I looked to the sky and watched birds fly overhead.

I breathed. I inhaled slowly. I exhaled slowly. I let myself feel my lungs inflate and deflate.

I let the sun hit my chest. I let my body find stillness. I let my thoughts and my frustrations fly away with those same birds.

When I got back on George, something incredible happened. He was calm and responsive. I hardly had to touch the reins.

He just moved with me. It wasn't training. It was an alignment, and I'll never forget it.

At first, I didn't even understand what energy meant in this context, but little by little, I began to notice how my tension showed up in my body, how even a clenched jaw or tightened shoulders could cause a horse to resist me. The more I softened, the more they did, too. It became a living feedback loop, a real-time reflection of how I was showing up in the world, not just with them but with my kids, my colleagues, and myself.

This was emotional intelligence in motion, not a theory from a book but a truth I could feel in my bones.

HEALING WITHOUT WORDS

There's something powerful about healing in silence.

At Warrior Ranch, I didn't have to explain myself. I didn't have to relive any trauma. I just had to be. I had to exist, show up, and, most importantly, be present. That's where the real work started, where the body and soul began to heal, even when the mind was still catching up. Over time, I transitioned into a leadership role at the ranch.

Now I help coach other veterans and first responders. I still work with the horses. I still feel the awe.

From my very first day there, they called me "the horse whisperer." I always just wanted to touch the horse. I always just wanted to be forehead to forehead with the horse.

I have always stared at the horse in awe, but now I also watch the faces of those I coach, those I guide. I can see their transformations.

Their posture shifts. Their eyes soften. I can feel and see their laughter return.

What used to be about my healing has now become about creating a space for others to find theirs: selfless service to others, just like my coaching girls' lacrosse.

I've been through years of traditional therapy. While I'm grateful for those conversations, I never felt like I was truly getting to the root. I talked about my pain, but I didn't feel it move. With horses, I didn't have to say a word, yet I felt something shift.

It was as if they bypassed my brain and connected straight with my heart.

PERFORMANCE TO PRESENCE

Working with horses taught me how to lead without force, how to influence with trust.

It changed how I did things. It changed how I parent, how I love, and how I lead my business. It's not about dominance anymore. It's about presence. It's about energy alignment. It's about love.

When I'm grounded, my kids feel it. My teammates feel it. My co-workers feel it. My fiancée feels it. I begin to see the thread in connecting, healing, and leadership. The best leaders don't bark orders. They create safety. They build trust. They hold space.

Most importantly, they lead with love, and that's what I'm learning to do. In the round pen, on the lacrosse field, at our dinner table, in the boardroom, that is what I do.

I recently had an experience that reminded me of the power of all of this. I was coaching a first responder, Steve. He reminded me of myself.

The first activity we do to promote connecting with the horse is grooming. One hand stays in physical contact with the horse while the other hand holds the brush and grooms. Connecting in silence helps you be present.

Steve could not stop talking during this time. You could hear and feel his nervous energy all over. He was so afraid to be present in the moment. He was so afraid to be vulnerable. So, the horse, feeling this, was very active and was becoming skittish as well, rocking its head up and down.

Typically, when you groom a horse, it's in a tremendous place of peace. And when a horse's head drops, that's when you know it's really calm.

Cody's head was doing everything but. We took a moment and told Steve to pause, drop the brush, and completely drape his body over the horse's body. Then we told him to be still, silence the noise, and breathe. I led him through breathing exercises, inhaling and exhaling, pausing at certain spots, allowing him to feel his chest sync with this horse.

As Steve released and relinquished control, we watched the weight of the world come off his shoulders. I watched him become vulnerable. I watched him become present. And the horse synced with him incredibly. Its head dropped, and it filled with calmness. It was beautiful.

The best part is learning to let go. It's learning how your presence within yourself truly defines selfishness versus self-care. The true power of awareness lies in understanding the journey inward, toward self-love and self-awareness.

It's crucial to differentiate between selfishness and self-care. For me, caring for myself is essential, not out of selfishness but as a necessity. When I am not at peace, I can't positively impact those around me. This understanding is vital—it's not about indulgence but about being the best version of myself. Only by aligning with inner peace and love can I truly be effective for others.

The journey inward enables me to love outwardly from a place of authenticity and compassion. If something disrupts this peace, I can't offer my best to the world. That's why this journey inward is so important—it's about being the best version of myself, not just for me but for others.

You don't have to talk your way into healing. Sometimes, the most powerful breakthroughs come in stillness, not speech. A thousand-pound animal can teach you more about trust, consistency, and leadership than a hundred self-help books.

If you're always trying to control things, maybe it's time to ask, what are you afraid will happen if you simply let go? Are you trying to force healing, or are you learning to receive it? Where in your life are you still trying to lead by control rather than influence? What would happen if you stopped bracing for rejection and started trusting your energy? How can you invite presence into your life, starting today? I invite you to pause. What does silence mean to you?

The horses taught me presence. They brought me to stillness. But something deeper still stirred within me—a calling beyond words, beyond form. I didn't know it yet, but my next teacher wouldn't walk on four legs. It would come from spirit—and it would completely break me open.

KEY TAKEAWAYS FROM CHAPTER 7

- **Healing doesn't always require words** – Some of the deepest breakthroughs come in silence, presence, and connection beyond language.
- **Horses reflect what we carry inside** – They don't care about your title or performance; they mirror your energy and invite you to become fully present.
- **True leadership isn't control—it's trust and alignment** – Whether you lead people, teams, or yourself, influence begins when you lead from grounded presence, not pressure.
- **Self-care is not selfish** – You cannot give your best to others if you are disconnected from yourself. Peace begins within.

- **Transformation often comes through unexpected teachers** – Sometimes, the path to wholeness looks nothing like what you expected.

YOUR REFLECTION CHALLENGE

Pause and consider the following:

1. Where are you trying to force outcomes in your life or leadership instead of trusting the process?

_____

_____

_____

2. What relationships could improve if you shifted from control to presence?

_____

_____

_____

3. What might silence reveal to you if you allowed yourself to sit with it?

_____

_____

_____

4. Are you mistaking busyness for healing? What would happen if you slowed down and truly *felt*?

_____

_____

_____

5. What is one small daily ritual you can commit to that reconnects you with your breath, your body, or your energy?

_____

_____

_____

Sometimes the bravest thing you can do is to **stop doing** and start **being**.

CHAPTER 8
BREAKING THE EGO: A SPIRITUAL AWAKENING

THE INVITATION THAT CHANGED EVERYTHING

t started with a text from my ex-wife: *"Bufo alvarius, 5-MeO-DMT, Mexico, you need to go."* I literally thought someone had stolen her phone.

I called her immediately. "What the hell are you talking about?" She told me how, strangely and unexpectedly, she'd kept running into veterans from Colorado to New York on trips, and each of them had talked about this sacred medicine and the healing that it brought.

None of it made sense to me at the time. I was extremely skeptical and dismissive. I thought she was crazy, but I do have a fantastic relationship with my ex-wife, so I agreed that I would research it.

I also told her this wasn't something a guy like me would ever do. And yet, despite everything I'd already been through, there was still an ache in my chest, something missing from my soul, a space that no amount of success, therapy, service, or even love could fill. I still carried a void.

So, I researched. I asked around. The more I listened, the more the idea began to make sense in a way that only the soul can truly understand.

I reached out to veterans in my network and asked them what they were doing. I asked them if they had ever heard of anything like this. They all had their own stories of their healing processes.

They also all told me collectively in group texts, *"Welcome to true healing. You're on the right path. Glad to see you breaking out of isolated attempts and finding your way. Keep going."*

Eventually, just as the universe brought me Fiona, I believe the universe brought me to Tandava Retreats. I scheduled a conversation with Joël and Victoria, the co-founders and the space holders of Tandava. I felt something I hadn't felt in a long time: a deep pull.

After speaking at length with them, I booked a retreat for Thanksgiving. It felt symbolic to me, as it was a time of gratitude, a time of release, and yet another time where I could try to reclaim myself.

About two months before the trip, Joël and Victoria emailed me a packet of information. It included a list of recommended readings and videos to watch. None of it was about actual medicine use. It was about spirituality, mind shifts, and intentionality in life.

One of the videos recommended was about a soldier whom the people wanted to protect from a neighboring army that was coming. So, they plastered gold over him as if he were a statue, and when the soldiers came by, they admired the statue and left it alone.

The invading army occupied the town and ruled over it, so the townspeople just left the soldier covered in gold armor, and everyone would come and look at and admire this beautiful statue.

Years went by. Finally, the army left the town, and the people chipped away the statue's gold layer. Underneath was the still-living soldier, who returned to the people in his true form, as his true self.

That hit home deeply. The gold that had been layered over the soldier was like the armor that had been built around me my whole life—this beautiful, shiny armor hand-plastered by society's external validation and praise. People saw this beautiful thing that they admired and constantly praised it, but underneath it was a lost person who didn't even know who he was anymore.

So, that became my intention. The need to find my calling back to myself.

ENTERING THE UNKNOWN: TEPOZTLÁN, MEXICO, TANDAVA RETREAT

During the five-hour flight and then the 90-minute cab ride from Mexico City to the sovereign town of Tepoztlán, I had plenty of time to let anxiety creep in. What was I doing?

I barely drink alcohol, yet I was flying to another country to surrender my mind to the most powerful psychedelic on earth, something called the "God molecule."

However, the moment I walked through the gates of Tandava, all that dissipated. The land felt sacred. The flowers and trees wrapped the retreat space beautifully. There was a Turkish sauna, a hot tub, and a grounding tree, which became my favorite place to sit in stillness. The energy of the land whispered, *You are safe here. This is a place for healing.*

On my first retreat, I met five other beautiful souls from all over the world: Vietnam, Guatemala, Chicago, and Denver. Each of us carried something. Each of us was ready to let go of something. Each of us was looking for something bigger.

My intentions were to forgive myself and let go of my past. I was on a quest to put all the pieces of the puzzle together and reclaim spirituality in my life.

Part of what I loved about Tandava Retreats, among all the places I researched, is that it was a place of healing for five days. It was not just about the medicine. Five days of healing, yoga, breathing exercises, mountain hikes, sound baths, temazcal ceremonies, and eating food fresh from the land.

It was a beautiful, sacred place for healing, with the benefit of being able to work with this medicine. They also make you call weeks before the trip to go over your intentions, your "why," your purpose. Then, after the retreat, you have weeks' worth of post-integration calls to see how your life is transforming after the retreat and how you are integrating your experience into your daily life.

FACING THE EGO: THE 5-MEO-DMT JOURNEY

No words can truly do justice to this experience. Joël and Victoria, my guides, my anchors, my angels, set the container inside a temple, unlike anything I'd ever stepped into: a sacred, glass-walled space surrounded by the mountains of Tepoztlán. It felt like the sky, mountains, and earth were meeting just for us.

Before the ceremony, they explained what was about to happen as best they could. "At some point in the journey, you may feel as though you are going to die," they said. "If that happens, let yourself die through surrender." Right before I inhaled this medicine, I was instructed to repeat three times, "I surrender. I am surrendering. I have surrendered."

Then I inhaled, lay back, and let go. Words fall short of explaining what it feels like to inhale 5-MeO-DMT. You dissolve in the process. No identity, no rank, no physical presence or awareness. No pain, no name, just vastness. You and your consciousness travel into unknown space and time, and then into everything.

The process allowed for up to three rounds of this sacred medicine. Each round was a deeply personal choice, with a simple hand gesture to Joël or Victoria indicating a desire to continue. This decision wasn't about physical strength or size but an inner calling, a recognition of whether there was more of the journey to explore.

Some would feel one dose was enough—a profound, earth-shattering, unworldly experience that left them fulfilled. Others might sense that their story needed more and feel compelled to journey further. It's an intuitive understanding, a knowing that guides you to seek more if you feel there's still a path to walk. Each round, a choice; each dose, a step deeper into self-discovery. It's not about endurance but about an innate sense of when your journey feels complete.

All I remember upon returning from my first journey was being in a puddle of tears, feeling like I was in a river, soaking wet, with no clue where it all came from. When I came back after my third and final round, I was also extremely hoarse. Later, I would learn more about what I'd gone through, the release, and the process of letting go.

After my first retreat, I stopped in Florida on the way back home to visit Ben, a dear brother of mine, whom I played Army lacrosse with and who lived in Boca Raton. A double amputee, he had suffered a traumatic injury in the special forces. While leading a patrol, he stepped on a road-side bomb and blew himself up. After major surgeries, spending time in a coma, and enduring multiple moments of flat-lining, he experienced a real-life death process.

At the end of a long day, we sat in his pool and spoke about everything, and we shared in great detail our death experiences, his real one and my fabricated one.

The similarities were mind-blowing and beautiful. Everything he described was exactly what I had experienced.

If I could describe the death process, understanding it is not a visual experience, but a feeling, and words fail to do any justice, it would be like this:

I felt myself, the physically strong, athletic man I've always been, hanging from a cliff. Above me stood my three children, reaching down, their eyes pleading: *Daddy, pull yourself up. Come back to us. We need you.*

On any ordinary day, a pull-up would be effortless. But in that moment, I realized—I couldn't do it. I had no strength, no control. I looked into their eyes, and I said something I never thought I would.

"I have to let go."

I didn't know what was going to happen when I let go. I didn't know what the fall was going to feel like. I didn't know what the impact of the fall would be, but I couldn't pull myself up. I had no power in this moment. I had absolutely no ability to control any of this. I had to let go.

There was nothing else I could do. And that newfound understanding, that we are in control of nothing, that we have no control of anything, was the greatest realization of my life.

The harder I gripped the cliff, the more I tried to pull myself up, the more I tried to control the situation, the more I failed. The only way to realize anything was to let go, no control, the ultimate death process.

As I fell, it felt like I was falling through universes.

Finally, I hit the floor on all fours, and there was a purge.

The purge was so strong that I felt like it lifted me back up so that I was floating, once again, in space. I purged embarrassment. I purged grief. I purged shame. I purged fear. I purged guilt. I purged childhood trauma and sexual, physical, and emotional abuse. It all came up from the deepest, darkest areas of my body, my life, where it had been so deeply buried.

I purged everything, and then I was back in the temple, and I had to try to process that. I just tried to embrace this feeling, this sense that I was nothing—yet everything, that I was one with the universe.

Finally, I stood and was escorted out of the temple and to the grounding tree by Joël and Victoria, where I continued to lie and just look up. I watched the leaves move in slow motion, listened to the birds chirping beautifully, and felt the warmth of the sun on my skin.

It was as if the universe were writing the script of everything so perfectly. A leaf, maybe 50 feet above, shed a drop of water that seemed to fall in slow motion. I watched the drop fall the entire way, and when it landed directly in the middle of my forehead, I giggled and told the universe to stop. There was no way that it could be that perfect.

From that experience, I realized what I had been longing for and missing: my calling back home to myself through a divine and spiritual connection.

Prior to this moment, I had been learning to love myself. I had been learning to be okay in my silence, but I still lacked spirituality. I had been learning to give of myself to something greater, to lead in selfless service, but I still hadn't fully understood the bigger picture. I hadn't believed in anything bigger.

And there it was: my connectedness to the universe. Spirituality returned to my life, right to my center.

It was a release of every burden. It was a reunion with something ancient and eternal inside of me. I was remembering a true connection, falling back to myself, to my center, to my light.

Every piece of armor was peeled away, and I felt safe to be vulnerable with no uniform, no protection. I needed nothing. I was perfect as I was.

And it had always been within me. I had searched so hard and fought for so many years for external validation. I had lived through the praise.

I had always felt a void within myself, one that had led to some of my breaking points. Now I realized that the void was an absence of spirituality, the disruption of my journey toward my internal light.

This experience unraveled everything I ever thought I knew about strength, independence, leadership, the universe, God, and myself.

And in its place was oneness. I wasn't a former soldier. I wasn't a product of abuse. I wasn't a divorced father. I wasn't broken.

I was creation itself, a divine expression of life, a soul finally freed, dancing in the now.

For the first time, I felt what it meant to be whole.

THE INTERNAL SHIFT FROM CONTROL TO TRUST

The ego screamed on the way out. Literally. I now knew why I was so hoarse after my third round with the medicine.

It didn't want to die. It did not want to surrender. It wanted to cling to titles, roles, and identities. It wanted to perform, to be validated. To be safe in the illusion of control.

But the medicine showed me that true strength lies not in control. True strength is in surrender.

For my whole life up until this moment, I had been a trained warrior. Surrender had never been in my vocabulary. But there I was, living proof that true strength is surrender.

The experience revealed to me the root of so much of my suffering. Not the trauma but the constant effort to manage it, manipulate it, and outrun it. The belief that if I just worked harder, led better, and loved more, I could finally be free.

However, freedom never comes from force. It comes from release.

When I returned home from Mexico, the world looked different. Softer. Slower. I found myself breathing more intentionally, listening more deeply, and loving more openly. I no longer needed to prove anything—not to others, not even to myself.

Something had shifted. The pace of life hadn't changed, but my presence within it had.

Then came the real work: integration. The transformation I had experienced wasn't meant to stay in the mountains of Mexico. It was meant to live in my everyday life. I began building new regimens—morning breathwork, quiet reflection, daily gratitude, and alignment between my words and actions. I stopped living for appearances and started living from within. And for the first time, success had nothing to do with achievement. It had everything to do with authenticity.

Once the embodiment of the alpha male stereotype—patriotic combat veteran with my American flag flying high—I found myself experiencing a profound sense of oneness. To symbolize this shift, I lowered my American flag in my front yard and replaced it with a dove crafted from the flags of every country across the globe.

This act was a testament to breaking down the barriers of geographic divides and embracing a universal love and connectedness. It was a symbol of recognizing that we are all one, bound by a shared humanity that transcends borders, and of embracing the energy of universal love.

I felt an overwhelming urge to share my newfound sense of purpose and healing with others. It was as if a fire had been kindled within me, driving me to illuminate the path to bliss for those still caught in their cycles.

However, I quickly realized that not everyone is ready or willing to embark on this inward journey. Some remain unaware of their need for healing, while others resist the light altogether. I learned that the most powerful way to inspire change was simply to be, to let my light shine by embodying the peace and joy I had found.

It was during this time that I nurtured my "spirituality tree," a fragile new growth that needed protection. I built boundaries around it, learning that while positivity attracts, it can also draw those who seek to diminish it. By standing firm in my light, I could offer a beacon for those truly ready to embark on their own journeys of transformation.

I read something that I now bring to my children, to my fiancée, and to people all the time. I simply ask, "What time is it?" They'll give me the time of day, and I'll ask again, "What time is it?"

The first time, maybe they rounded to 3:30, so now they'll say, "It's 3:33?"

"No," I tell them, "the time is now."

Then I'll ask, "Where are we?"

"At lacrosse practice?" they might say. "At work? In the kitchen?"

"No," I'll answer, "we are here."

The only thing that matters is the here and now. That level of presence will change everything.

Yesterday serves you no purpose, whether it was good or bad, and tomorrow is not promised. The only thing we are promised is the here and now.

Be present in everything you do. When you are having a conversation with someone, are you wondering about something else and not truly listening? Are you present in every single moment? Because that is all we are promised. By being present, you will soon understand that there are no ordinary moments.

I finally realized something that I live by every single day: we cannot control our outcomes, but we can control our outlook. That realization, if you truly embody it, is so empowering.

One of the easiest illustrations of this is the weather.

I have no control over whether the sun will shine tomorrow or if it will rain, but I have all the control in the world over my outlook on whether it's a sunny or rainy day. If, on a rainy day, I sulk and I'm not happy because it's a gray sky, I am responsible for that, not the weather. You have the ability to control your outlook.

You can still choose to live in a place of gratitude, of appreciating what the actual rain means for living organisms and for the earth and other things. You can choose the power to control your outlook, but you will never be able to control outcomes. Once you realize that, your daily living becomes so much easier.

THE IMPORTANCE OF BREATH

Breath is a bridge between the mind and the heart, not just a relaxation tool.

It's a lifeline, a portal to the present moment. I spent much of my life engaged in shallow breathing, racing, waiting for the next hit, the next trigger, the next expectation. Now, I pause, sit, and breathe.

I use box breathing, the Wim Hof method, and much more while grounding my bare feet into the earth. My breath reminds me that I'm alive, that I'm safe, and that I'm returning to my home.

This is the medicine I carry into my everyday life, into my parenting, into my business, into love. The breath doesn't lie. It always brings you back to truth.

You're already doing it thousands of times a day, but what if you could do it with intention? Inhale clarity; exhale chaos. That's the power of breath. If your thoughts feel scattered, your chest tight, and your nerves frayed, then pause and breathe. Just breathe.

It's more powerful than you think. When was the last time you took a deep, intentional breath? What emotions are you holding in your breath right now? Can you take five slow, deep breaths and notice how your thoughts shift?

This is where everything started to shift for me. My spiritual awakening wasn't the end of my story. It was the beginning of a conscious life built on love, alignment, and truth.

The next step was to return home, not just to my life but to myself.

KEY TAKEAWAYS FROM CHAPTER 8

- **True freedom isn't control—it's surrender**
- You don't find yourself by gripping tighter, but by letting go of the illusion that you can control outcomes.
- **Your identity isn't your title, your success, or your past**
- Who you *are* has always been deeper than what you *do*. You are already worthy.
- **Spirituality isn't outside you—it lives within you**
- You don't need to search the world for meaning. You carry the light you're looking for.
- **The only time is *now***
- Peace lives in the present moment, not in the past you can't change or the future you can't control.
- **Breath is your anchor to presence**
- Every inhale and exhale is a bridge between your mind and your heart, pulling you back to the here and now.
- **Outlook is everything**
- You may not control what happens, but you *always* control how you respond.
- **The path to peace begins when you stop performing and start *being***
- You don't have to impress anyone to be enough. You already are.

YOUR REFLECTION CHALLENGE

Pause and consider the following:

1. Where in your life are you gripping the cliff, trying to control what's already asking to be surrendered?

_____

_____

_____

2. Are you performing for validation or living from alignment?

_____

_____

_____

3. What mask are you finally ready to lay down?

_____

_____

_____

4. What does surrender look like for you—not as giving up, but as letting go of what no longer serves you?

_____

_____

_____

5. When was the last time you slowed down to notice your breath, the present moment, or the miracle of simply being alive?

_____

_____

_____

6. What would it feel like to stop chasing worth and start trusting that you already *are* enough, here and now?

_____

_____

_____

"The time is now. You are already home."

CHAPTER 9
LOVE, EXPANSION, AND THE NEXT CHAPTER

MEETING THE LOVE OF MY LIFE

After years of healing and working inward, I learned to create boundaries and make changes in my life to remove myself from certain relationships and situations. One of those changes was switching to a new gym. That's when I first saw Kathryn. Though I didn't know it yet, she had recently made a change in her gym schedule from nights to mornings, allowing us to meet. Her presence was magnetic, based on something more than physical beauty.

As I passed her, I mumbled, "You should wear those braids in your hair more often. It's very motivating."

"Yeah, I get that a lot," she casually replied and then kept walking.

I couldn't let that be the end of our exchanges. There was something about her energy, her light, that was so powerful and such a draw. I pursued any conversation I could with her.

Something inside of me knew. Right after my first conversation with Kathryn, I texted my best friend, Diana, *"I just met the woman I want to marry."*

At that point in my life, I had made peace with never marrying again, and with three amazing teenagers, the thought of having more children never entered my mind. But Kathryn was something different. She was the living proof of the work I had done.

My connection through selfless service and witnessing others be lifted, my understanding of my need for connection to nature and the sun, my time working with horses, my time at Tandava Retreats—it all allowed me the space to feel and brought me to a higher level of awareness toward the connection of energy.

Every time I looked at Kathryn, that is what I saw. The light I had uncovered inside myself was reflected in her energy. It wasn't about her appearance. It was about energy, presence, alignment, and oneness.

Every interaction with her felt like two souls finally reconnecting. Within a few weeks of meeting, I hand-wrote her a two-page letter, pouring out my feelings and my vision for a shared future. She brought it to her younger sister, who, like any protective sibling, was cautious and warned her about being able to trust this situation.

But I knew that what I felt wasn't too much. It was everything. It was the culmination of my entire life's journey, leading me to the highest human experience: love.

Our first few weeks together weren't perfect, and they weren't easy. Kathryn, like me, carried the weight of old wounds. The residue of past relationships, betrayals, and heartbreaks caused her to question the realness of what we were building. A few times, she pulled away, not because she didn't feel something, but because she did, and the intensity of it scared her. She wasn't sure if she could trust something that felt this safe, this aligned.

I didn't take it personally. I saw her. I saw the part of her that wanted to stay but feared being hurt again. So, each time she walked away, I stayed present. I reminded her that I was here, not just as a man who loved her but as her best friend. I wasn't going anywhere. I told her I would earn her trust, not with words but with unwavering presence. My love wasn't conditional on her certainty. I loved her for her past, for who she was in the moment, and for everything she was still becoming.

Five months later, I dropped to one knee on a mountaintop in Switzerland and proposed. We set the wedding date for exactly one year later and began planning our life and the sharing of our dreams of having children together.

A RELATIONSHIP BUILT ON ENERGY, PRESENCE, AND INTENTION

Kathryn had undergone her own healing journey. After suffering childhood trauma and a broken relationship with her father, she had found a path to peace by hiking mountains around the world.

She taught me to zoom out, see life with perspective, and feel small in a beautiful, freeing way. We built our relationship on intention, awareness, emotional honesty, and unconditional love. We saw each other with depth and clarity.

My first marriage followed the expected path: young love, college, marriage, children, and the first home with the white picket fence. But I lacked the tools, awareness, and emotional safety to make it work. In fact, at the time, I didn't even know that I needed them.

With Kathryn, it was different. She didn't complete me. She met me at my wholeness.

My relationship with Kathryn is not only a testament to my second chance at life but also to my understanding of what it truly means to appreciate happiness. Some might believe that happiness is only real when it's shared. And while my growth taught me not to rely on Kathryn for my happiness, it also allowed me to live in a space acknowledging how special it is to share happiness as a testimony to each other's existence.

I tell her all the time, "You don't make me happy. I make me happy. You don't make me feel so loved. I make me feel so loved. But you add so much to my being happy and being loved in a way that brings me to absolute bliss."

What makes this love so sacred is that it didn't just arrive. It was earned through growth, pain, and healing. We each had to go through our own dark nights of the soul. We had to shed the versions of ourselves that were built to survive. We had to grieve, forgive, surrender, and rebuild. Only then, only after doing the work, could we be trusted with a love this real.

This relationship is more than timing. It is divine alignment, a gift from God, from the universe, from something far greater than ourselves. If it had shown up any sooner, we wouldn't have been able to recognize it or receive it. We weren't ready until we were whole. We didn't find each other in our brokenness. We found each other in our becoming.

SPIRITUAL GROWTH TOGETHER

When I shared my profound spiritual experiences at Tandava Retreats in Tepoztlán, Mexico, with Kathryn, she immediately expressed a desire to go with me.

Experiencing 5-MeO-DMT alone was transformational, but experiencing it together was divine. In that sacred temple, side by side, we surrendered, trusted, and witnessed each other's healing.

That moment deepened not just our romantic connection but our spiritual bond. We held space for each other, supported each other's pain, and loved without conditions. It became a foundation for our way of life: daily, intentional, and filled with emotional connection, gratitude, presence, and purpose.

We do breathwork together. We meditate together, understanding that our spiritual bond and quality time together serve a much higher purpose.

From that shared space of healing emerged not just transformation but a lifelong bond with Joël and Victoria, the two divine guides who helped me rediscover my soul. What they offered me in stillness, presence, and trust now extends to Kathryn, too, as we walk this path together. They are more than facilitators. They are mirrors of wisdom, walking examples of compassion and presence, and the relationship we now share with them is a gift that continues to nourish our lives well beyond the mountains of Tepoztlán.

What we discovered together wasn't just love. It was unity, the kind that can only be felt when two people are spiritually aligned, when they are grounded not in fantasy but in truth. In oneness. In soul awareness.

When two people are individually connected to a source and then come together, what forms between them is not just a relationship. It is a sacred space. A sanctuary. A mirror of divine potential.

Spiritual alignment between partners doesn't make life perfect. It makes life deep. It opens a channel for communication that goes beyond words. It creates a resonance, a harmony that's felt in silence, in the still-ness, in the shared breath before sleep.

I use the metaphor of a table to describe a healthy relationship. It has four strong legs: emotional, spiritual, physical, and financial. If any leg weakens, the table wobbles. The metaphor guides our relationship. Each leg gets daily attention.

Our love became a prayer, not just for each other but for how we show up in the world, for how we raise our future children. We walk this life together, yes, but also as a whole. Sovereign beings doing their work side by side.

We see our union not just as a blessing but as a responsibility to keep growing, to keep awakening, and to keep choosing each other, not from need but from sacred knowing.

THE MOUNTAIN METAPHOR: PERSPECTIVE ON PROBLEMS

Before Kathryn, my idea of a vacation was going to an all-inclusive resort on any Caribbean island. She changed that. Just a few months into our relationship, we embarked on a journey through Italy and Switzerland. For ten days, we were side by side, navigating new countries, overcoming language barriers, and driving through unfamiliar roads.

One particular instance during a long road trip stood out: the highway was completely closed, and we faced hours of detours and language barriers that prevented us from having any understanding of where we were or where we needed to go. Not once did we let frustration seep in. Instead, we embraced each wrong turn as it added hours, not minutes, to the trip with love and patience, knowing that the essence of our vacation was the time we spent together. It was this unwavering pres-ence and understanding that highlighted the depth of our connection.

I remember one hike in particular, climbing step by step in silence before reaching the summit. The view from the top shifted something in me. From up there, my biggest problems seemed so small, the pain of the past a distant echo. That climb wasn't just physical; it was symbolic: one step at a time, one choice at a time, one day at a time, and suddenly, you're looking at life from a whole new angle.

Peace doesn't come when your problems disappear. It comes when your perspective shifts.

A few months later, another trip exemplified our love. Our trip to Norway was meant to be a grand adventure, meticulously planned with every detail in place, but when my fiancée's passport wasn't valid for the required period, we found ourselves turned away at the airport.

In a moment that could have been charged with frustration and disappointment, we embraced the situation with calm and understanding. Taking the setback in stride, we found a way to get her a new passport the next day, rebooked flights, Airbnbs, rental cars, and adjusted our plans. We lost a lot of money, but we remained united, never once blaming each other, but rather supporting one another.

It was a testament to our bond, showing that our presence together was the most important aspect of any journey. Even when faced with challenges, we found joy in our time together, proving that the essence of our love lies in our unity, not in the places we visit.

A NEW KIND OF FATHERHOOD

Today, I am blessed with a deep, loving connection with my three children. They're the ultimate proof of my journey.

They've seen who I was and who I've become. It wasn't linear. There were setbacks. But there was much more growth and, above all, so much love. Still, I often wish that I had known then what I know now. I don't live with regret, but I do reflect.

That reflection fuels my excitement to become a father again with Kathryn. We're building a life rooted in intention, truth, and emotional presence, a life where our children will be welcomed into the world by two souls who have done the work, who have chosen love, growth, and purpose.

I think about the man I was the night I almost ended my life, and I think about the man I am today. The contrast is staggering. One version of me was ready to surrender to the pain. The other chose a deeper surrender—the kind that breaks the ego and births awareness.

This isn't just a second chance at fatherhood. This is a second chance at life. There was a time when I truly believed that I had nothing left to give. The weight was too much, and the pain was too loud. Yet, here I am, breathing, loving, creating, holding my children, building a future, waking up with gratitude.

So, if you're reading this and you're stuck in the spiral, if you feel like the pain will never end, like the silence inside your own mind is unbearable, I need you to know something. You are not broken. You are not alone. And this isn't the end of your story.

Healing is real. Redemption is real. And the life you've dreamed of, one of peace, connection, and purpose, is still possible. You can choose life. You can choose healing. You can choose love.

You don't have to stay stuck in patterns that no longer serve you. You don't have to carry the weight of your past into your future. There is a new way to live, to love, to show up for yourself and the people around you.

This is my second chance, and I'm holding it with gratitude. If I could find it, you can, too. Love doesn't show up when you're perfect. It shows up when you're honest, present, and ready to receive it.

Healing doesn't just change your relationship with yourself. It changes how you connect with everyone else. What if your next chapter isn't about fixing yourself but about expanding into who you already are? There's something sacred about being ready, truly ready, for love, peace, and purpose.

Are you truly open to receiving the love you say you want, or are you still blocking it with old wounds? What would it look like to show up in your relationships fully, without the mask, without the fear? What impact do you want to leave through your relationships with your spouse, your kids, and your community? What's one area of your life where you can choose expansion over fear?

Love grounded me. Perspective elevated me. Healing expanded me. But now it was time to channel everything I had learned, every scar, every lesson, every ounce of truth, into something that would serve as many as I could reach in my professional life.

KEY TAKEAWAYS FROM CHAPTER 9

- **True love meets you when you meet yourself**
- Kathryn didn't complete me—she reflected the wholeness I had already fought to reclaim.
- **Love is not something you earn—it's something you *receive***
- When two whole people come together, they create not dependency, but divine partnership.
- **Spiritual alignment deepens love beyond words**
- It's not about being perfect for each other, but about holding space to keep growing, healing, and expanding together.
- **Peace doesn't come from avoiding problems, but from shifting your perspective on them**
- Whether climbing a mountain or navigating life's detours, the view always changes when you do.
- **Presence transforms relationships more than any grand gesture ever could**
- Love isn't built in milestones, but in the quiet, consistent choice to show up every single day.
- **Your second chance isn't a reset—it's a sacred responsibility**

- The life you're building now becomes the impact you leave on those you love.
- **Healing changes how you *show up* for love, leadership, and life itself**
- Your journey toward self-awareness and peace isn't just for you—it's for every life you touch.

YOUR REFLECTION CHALLENGE

1. Are you open to receiving love without needing to perform for it?

   _____

   _____

   _____

2. What relationships in your life need more presence, not more effort?

   _____

   _____

   _____

3. Are you still waiting for life to feel perfect before you allow yourself to love fully?

_____

_____

_____

4. What would change if you believed you were already enough to deserve the love, peace, and connection you desire?

_____

_____

_____

5. Where can you practice shifting your perspective today, turning a problem into an opportunity for expansion?

_____

_____

_____

6. What impact of love, presence, and purpose are you choosing to leave behind—starting now?

_____

_____

_____

"Your greatest love story begins when you come home to yourself."

CHAPTER 10
THE BUSINESS JOURNEY BEGINS

THE SHIFT FROM CORPORATE SUCCESS TO PERSONAL FULFILLMENT

After all the pain that I had processed, after all the healing work, all the reflection, there came a moment when I realized that something big had shifted inside me.

My definition of success had changed.

I had chased promotions like they were proof of my worth, and I'd worn my job titles like armor. I believed that the longer I stayed at the office, the better father I was becoming because I was providing, and that was validated by promotions and praise.

But providing without presence isn't love; it's a transaction. The high-performing corporate career looked great on paper, with bonuses, recognition, and stability, but underneath that success was a quiet, relentless ache.

I had buried my trauma under deadlines, hiding in meetings and winning quarterly awards while losing myself with a lack of purpose. I'd been rewarded for being emotionally numb, rewarded for overworking, rewarded for pain that I never talked about because it looked like drive and success to everyone else.

The foundation of my new definition of success was formulated by my journey back to spirituality and knowing that happiness and presence far outweighed anything big companies had to offer. Any other version of me no longer existed.

THE DECISION TO START MY OWN BUSINESS

Through my healing journey, clarity emerged: I couldn't keep giving my best energy to building someone else's dreams while robbing myself and my family of the best parts of me. I also promised to live every day with intentionality. Part of that intention was holding my second chance at life with sacred gratitude. I vowed to be more present in my life, my fiancée's life, and our children's lives, current and future.

I had climbed the corporate ladder and proven myself, but the next promotion couldn't fix the emptiness I felt. I had fixed that myself, so I knew it was time for me to take the leap. Change doesn't happen by staying comfortable. True change occurs by forcing ourselves to be uncomfortable.

Leaving corporate wasn't comfortable. It wasn't easy. There was fear, uncertainty, pressure, and the unknown. But underneath all that, there was peace in knowing that I was choosing my values over validation, peace in knowing that I was about to build something from the inside out, peace in building something and succeeding for myself, not for someone else's betterment.

I prayed. I planned. I trusted that all my skills, especially the leadership skills that I had developed through sports, war, and trauma, were not meant to die in a boardroom. They were meant to build something different, something aligned, something whole.

BUILDING A BUSINESS AROUND PRESENCE AND PURPOSE

When I built my business, I didn't start with strategy—I started with values.

- Work-life balance
- Presence with my kids and my fiancée
- Leading with integrity
- Creating a culture of trust and love

I made a promise to myself.

I would never again miss the moments that mattered. I would coach my kids' teams. I would show up to their events. I would stop at my fiancée's job and bring her flowers or take her to lunch. I would no longer live for Fridays and wake up dreading Mondays.

This business wasn't just about income. It was about impact.

It wasn't about status. It was about service.

It wasn't built for vanity. It was built for value. It was built with the purpose of helping people.

Starting my own business was rooted in defining what success truly meant for me. It wasn't just about financial metrics but about achieving a work-life balance that allowed me to live more presently.

I carefully forecasted my finances and decided that my goal wasn't just to break even or maximize profits but to create a fulfilling lifestyle. This meant valuing presence over performance and impact over mere numbers.

While I prioritized work-life balance, I also recognized that my team might have different definitions of success, and I embraced this diversity. By fostering a culture that allowed each person to pursue their own path to fulfillment, I built a business grounded in shared values and personal growth, where success was measured not just by the bottom line but by the quality of life it provided.

THE LEADERSHIP EVOLUTION

Since high school, I have occupied positions of leadership. In sports, I led through performance.

In the military, I led through courage. In the corporate world, I led through pressure. Now, though, I lead with impact and presence.

One of the greatest leadership traits I've ever learned is consistency. Not perfection, consistency. I had a regional manager who was a great example of inconsistency. All employees waited every day for this manager to walk through the front doors. The job itself brought enough stress to us every day, but this moment could either add more stress and anger or not.

If our regional manager walked through those doors with his sunglasses on top of his head, we were going to be okay. If he walked through those front doors with his sunglasses still covering his eyes, we knew it was going to be that much longer of a day.

People don't follow flawless leaders. They follow leaders who show up again and again, consistently and genuinely, and who have their people's best interests at heart. I've learned that love belongs in leadership. I set boundaries with compassion. People want accountability.

They want to know what they are doing well and what they can be doing better. I build a culture where people feel seen, heard, and valued. I lead firmly, but with heart.

I've seen firsthand how emotional regulation, calm decision-making, and trust-building shape not just company performance but people's lives. In business, just like in life, things will go wrong. Problems arise.

No amount of overreacting, shouting, or getting upset will change the facts. I stay consistent through the good news and the bad. I also create a culture and environment where you do not have to be a leader or a manager to help create solutions.

When all people are seen, all are heard, and all are valued, everyone feels empowered to be a part of the solutions.

THE REWARD IS PRESENCE

Starting my business gave me something far more valuable than ownership. It gave me presence. Now I coach my kids without worrying about how I will make up time at the office. I'm at their school events without having to take PTO. I sit with them at dinner, say a few words of gratitude, and never check my phone for work emails or customer texts. I laugh more. I listen more. I feel more.

The business gave me income. The healing gave me my life back. It wasn't easy. The road here was brutal. But it was worth every scar, every fall, every sleepless night because, today, I'm not just a business owner. I'm a father who's present, a partner who's awake, and a man who finally knows who he is, who always leads with love.

You can chase titles, promotions, and salaries, but what are you sacrificing in the process? Success means nothing if it costs you your peace, your purpose, or your presence. What if your greatest contribution to the world isn't what you do but how you do it and who you become along the way?

You don't have to start a business to live in alignment, but you do have to decide: What are you building, and is it worth your life? Are you living accordingly? Are you living according to your values or just reacting to expectations? What does success actually mean to you now in this season? If you could build your life around what truly matters, what would need to change? What are you willing to risk to live in alignment with your purpose?

Building a life aligned with your values is just the beginning. Living that life with presence, peace, and purpose day after day is true fulfillment. That's where the real wisdom lies.

KEY TAKEAWAYS FROM CHAPTER 10

- **True success is built on presence, not promotions**
- You don't have to sacrifice your peace or your family to prove your worth.
- **You are not here to build someone else's dream at the expense of your own**
- Your purpose deserves your full energy, not your leftovers.
- **Leadership is about consistency, not perfection**
- People don't follow titles; they follow trust.
- **A values-driven life will always feel richer than a performance-driven one**
- Alignment, not achievement, is the real win.
- **Presence is the greatest reward any work can give you**
- Being fully alive in your own life is more meaningful than any paycheck.
- **You don't have to quit your job to live in alignment, but you do have to choose**
- Living with intention requires clarity, courage, and daily action.
- **True fulfillment is built in the ordinary moments, not the highlight reels**
- How you show up—consistently and with love—is what people will remember.

YOUR REFLECTION CHALLENGE

1. What's your current definition of success? Has it changed?

   _____

   _____

   _____

2. Are you living your life in alignment with your deepest values —or someone else's expectations?

   _____

   _____

   _____

3. What parts of your life have you built around validation instead of purpose?

   _____

   _____

   _____

4. How do you define leadership—not as a title, but as a way of being?

_____

_____

_____

5. Where can you lead more with presence and love, both at work and at home?

_____

_____

_____

6. What's one small change you can make this week to bring more alignment between how you live and what you truly value?

_____

_____

_____

7. If you could design your life around what truly matters, what would it look like?

_____

_____

_____

"The real reward isn't the business you build. It's the life you choose to live fully awake."

CHAPTER 11

GOLD NUGGETS OF WISDOM: CHOOSING PEACE, PURPOSE, AND TRUE FULFILLMENT

REDEFINING SUCCESS AND LIVING BY STANDARDS

When I graduated from West Point, I believed that success meant power, prestige, and rising to the top.

I thought the goal was to wear a fancy suit, sit in a corner office, and eventually become the CEO of some major corporation. I believed that this was the only way to honor my education, my experience, and my worth. That is how I would know that I had made it.

Now I know better. Today, my definition of success has completely shifted. Success isn't status. It's peace. It's presence. It's purpose. It's laughing with my kids, holding hands with my fiancée, and doing meaningful work that aligns with my values.

Real leadership doesn't start in a boardroom. It starts within and then at home. It starts with how I show up for my children, how I communicate with my partner, and how I hold space for myself when things feel heavy.

Success is not trying to be remembered by the people who signed my paycheck or offered me a promotion. Success is self-love. Success is being remembered by the people who matter most.

BREAKING GENERATIONAL TRAUMA

One of the greatest honors of my life is the way my ex-wife and I choose to co-parent.

We made a conscious decision to break the generational cycles of pain. We agreed that no matter what, we would always treat each other with respect. We would never insult each other in front of our children.

We would hold each other in the highest regard and raise our children with mutual love and emotional maturity. That decision changed everything. We can pass down pain, or we can pass down peace.

That's the choice. My healing didn't just impact me. I wasn't just healing for myself. It became a pathway for my children, so I was also healing for them. By facing my pain, I was giving them permission to create a life built on love instead of fear. They found strength in my vulnerability.

Imagine the stillness of a serene pond, undisturbed and calm. Now picture a single stone dropped into its center. The ripples spread outward, touching everything in their path. When we are caught in anger and frustration, these emotions are like stones creating ripples that affect not just us but everyone around us. The energy we emit influences those in our vicinity, creating a chain reaction that can reach far beyond what we initially perceive.

However, when we do the inner work, when we heal and find peace within ourselves, the stones we cast into the water are gentle. The ripples of love, understanding, and compassion extend in the same way, touching lives and bringing peace.

This is the power of our inner state—like ripples in water, our actions and emotions radiate outward, influencing the world around us. When we come from a place of inner peace and love, the ripples we create can change not only our lives but the lives of those around us, echoing far beyond what we can imagine.

My children saw the power in my softness. They felt unconditional love in ways I once hadn't known how to give, and through that, they began to heal, too.

YOU GET TO LIVE TWICE

There's a saying I've come to live by. You get to live twice. The second life begins when you awaken to the truth that life isn't happening to you. It's unfolding within you, and presence is our most sacred gift.

This is my second life. I don't take a moment of it for granted.

I'm in a new relationship rooted in intention and deep presence. I have the opportunity to raise future children from a starting space of peace, wisdom, and open-hearted love. I've built a business not on status or validation, but on service and soul.

I wake up with clarity, purpose, and gratitude. I reflect often. I almost threw it all away, but look at me now.

That's the miracle of choosing to stay.

THE POWER OF SHARED HAPPINESS

American adventurer and wanderer Christopher McCandless once wrote, *"Happiness is only real when shared."*[1] For the longest time, I didn't understand this.

I thought it meant that I needed others to complete me. I thought it meant dependency, but now I understand. Healing taught me to love inward first, to be whole before trying to give myself to another. Now that I know how to hold that love, I can share it, truly share it, without needing, without clinging, just offering.

---

1. Jon Krakauer, *Into the Wild* (New York: Anchor, 1997), 141.

The pursuit of healing wasn't just about me. It was so I could love and be fully loved, genuinely and fiercely. That growth prepared me to connect more deeply with my kids, my fiancée, my community, and, most importantly, myself.

True happiness is found in connection, and real connection starts with honesty, both with yourself and others.

CALL TO REFLECT AND RISE

You've made it to this page for a reason.

Something in you is waking up. Don't ignore it. No matter how far gone you think you are, there is a way back to purpose.

You are not a victim. You are not your trauma. You are not your mistakes, and you are not too late.

Your future doesn't have to look like your past, but only you can decide to write a new story. The pen is in your hand.

CLOSING REFLECTIONS: COMING HOME TO YOURSELF

I used to believe that healing would come from somewhere outside of me, a promotion, a paycheck, a partner, a moment where everything would click and I'd finally feel whole, but the truth is that it didn't come from out there. It came the moment I turned inward, the moment I closed my eyes and finally sat with myself, the moment I listened to my breath and not the noise, the moment I stopped running and decided to listen.

What I found in the silence wasn't perfection. It wasn't clear right away. It was pain, confusion, and doubt, but beneath that, beneath the noise and the fear, I found *me*.

I found the version of myself that had always been there, the one who was buried beneath the armor, the one who had walked with me through every storm, the one who whispered keep going, even when I didn't want to.

What I've learned is this: You don't have to earn your worth. You don't have to chase peace. You don't have to become someone else to be loved. You just have to remember who you already are.

The truest version of you isn't broken. It's buried beneath the roles, expectations, wounds, and noise. Once you decide to go within, to really go within, you will begin to uncover the greatest truth of all: that you've always been enough, that your presence is powerful, that your purpose is already alive within you, that peace is not a destination.

Peace is a practice, a choice, a breath. So, when life feels heavy, when the world pulls you in every direction, when your mind tells you that you're lost or unworthy, come back home. Close your eyes. Put your hand over your heart. And remember, you are not the pain you've endured. You are the light that survived it.

You are not the mistakes you've made. You are the wisdom those mistakes taught you. You are not a project to fix.

You are a soul to love. And no matter what happens next in your story, you will always have access to the most important relationship you'll ever have: the one with yourself.

Let that be the light you ignite in others. Let that be your peace. Let that be your purpose.

What story do you want your life to tell from this point forward? What does peace actually look like in your life? And what's standing in the way? Who will benefit if you choose to heal? Who will suffer if you don't? What are the core values you want to build your life on now?

To anyone who feels there's no way forward, who's overwhelmed by the weight of it all, my advice is simple: stop, sit down, and breathe. Feel the air flowing into your lungs and out again. In that breath, find the reminder that you are alive. And if you are alive, there is always a chance for things to get better. Life itself is an opportunity, a chance to rewrite your story.

Take one small step forward—then another. Go one day at a time, and in each day, find intentionality in your actions. This is how change is created—by building something better, step by step, breath by breath. Remember, it's not over. The best is yet to come, and you have the power to embrace it. I'm living proof that even from the lowest points, you can rebuild, find joy, and live a second life full of possibility.

Your healing is your power. Your presence is your purpose. You've survived what was meant to break you.

Now, it's time to build what you were born to create.

Chip away the armor. Come home to yourself in the name of love.

KEY TAKEAWAYS FROM CHAPTER 11

- **Success is no longer about status—it's about peace, presence, and purpose.**
- True success is measured by how fully you live, not how high you climb.
- **Healing doesn't stop with you—it creates ripples that impact generations.**
- The energy you bring into your relationships can either repeat cycles of pain or create cycles of peace.
- **You get to live twice—the second life begins when you realize you have the power to rewrite your story.**
- Awareness is the doorway to your second chance.
- **Happiness isn't dependency—it's wholeness shared.**
- When you love yourself first, you can give and receive love without needing it to fill a void.
- **The life you want is already within reach—but only if you stop chasing and start choosing.**
- You don't have to fix yourself. You have to come home to yourself.

- **Presence is the most powerful impact you can leave.**
- Every breath is an invitation to live fully, love deeply, and lead authentically.

FINAL REFLECTION CHALLENGE

1. What story do you want to tell from this day forward?

_____

_____

_____

2. What does peace actually *look* and *feel* like in your life?

_____

_____

_____

3. What's standing in the way of the life you know you're meant to live?

_____

_____

_____

4. Who benefits if you choose to heal—and who might suffer if you don't?

_____

_____

_____

5. What are the core values you want to root your life in now, not someday?

_____

_____

_____

6. What is one small, actionable step you can take today to chip away the armor and come home to yourself?

_____

_____

_____

"You've already survived what tried to break you. Now it's time to build what you were born to create."

CONCLUSION

CHOOSE PURPOSE, BREAK CYCLES, REDEEM TIME

You've just walked through my story.

It's not a straight line or a highlight reel, but the full spectrum: trauma, war, numbness, achievement, collapse, love, loss, silence, and, finally, awakening. But this was never just my story.

This book was a mirror, a reflection of the universal human experience. The masks we wear. The pain we bury. The love we crave. The peace we forget is available to us, always, in the here and now. If you've made it to this page, then you already know this.

This book wasn't about sports, the military, business, or fatherhood. It was about what happens when someone loses everything outside themselves and finally uncovers what was inside all along. Not perfection, not performance, but presence and purpose.

Time is the most sacred gift we can give, and you gave yours to me. Thank you. My prayer is that I gave something in return.

Maybe it was a breath of clarity, a new lens, or simply the reminder that you're not alone. The truth is, this isn't just about healing the past. It's about reclaiming your present moment and your future.

It's a different kind of success. I used to think that success meant proving something to others and to myself. Now, I believe that success is something else entirely.

Success means to live fully. To love openly. To walk in alignment with who you really are when no one is watching.

You can't go back and change your story, but you can take authorship of the chapter ahead. What time is it—now? Why are we—here? That's all we ever have, and that's everything we need. The impact you choose.

You're not healing just for you. You're healing for those who came before you and those who will come after. Your ancestors or your parents may not understand your path, but your children will feel the difference. They will grow up not under the weight of your trauma but under the light of your transformation.

Let that be your living contribution: not perfection, but intention.

One final truth: You get to live twice.

The second life begins when you remember that wholeness isn't something to achieve but something to return to. Not through force, but through stillness, through grace, through remembering who you are beneath the armor.

Take off the mask. Chip away the armor. Come home to yourself and build something beautiful from the ashes.

And if you're ready for more, if this book stirred something in you, if you're feeling the call to go deeper into your healing, purpose, or leadership, I would be honored to walk that path with you.

I speak to veteran groups, professional organizations and businesses, athletic teams, and individuals who are ready to live, lead, and love. Let's turn pain into purpose and story into strength. Let's stop performing and start becoming.

There are no ordinary moments. This is your only time.
You are not broken. You are breaking through.

THANK YOU FOR READING MY BOOK!

DOWNLOAD YOUR FREE GIFTS

Just to say thanks for buying and reading my book, I would like to give you a few free bonus gifts!

Scan the QR Code:

I appreciate your interest in my book and value your feedback as it helps me improve future versions. I would appreciate it if you could leave your invaluable review on Amazon.com with your feedback. Thank you!

.

www.ingramcontent.com/pod-product-compliance
Lightning Source LLC
Chambersburg PA
CBHW020203090426
42734CB00008B/927